Meeting the Needs
of Your Most Able Pupils:
PHYSICAL EDUCATION
and SPORT

Other titles in the series

Meeting the Needs of Your Most Able Pupils: Art
Kim Earle
1 84312 331 2

Meeting the Needs of Your Most Able Pupils: Design and Technology
Louise T. Davies
1 84312 330 4

Meeting the Needs of Your Most Able Pupils: Music
Jonathan Savage
1 84312 347 9

Meeting the Needs

of Your Most Able Pupils:

PHYSICAL EDUCATION
and SPORT

David Morley and Richard Bailey

David Fulton Publishers

David Fulton Publishers Ltd
The Chiswick Centre, 414 Chiswick High Road, London W4 5TF

www.fultonpublishers.co.uk
www.onestopeducation.co.uk

David Fulton Publishers is a division of Granada Learning Limited, part of ITV plc.

British Library Cataloguing in Publication Data
A catalogue record for this book is available from the British Library.

ISBN: 1 84312 334 7

10 9 8 7 6 5 4 3

Series production editor: Andrew Welsh
Typeset by Servis Filmsetting Ltd, Manchester
Printed and bound in Great Britain

To Dawn, Zara and Imogen, let's smell the roses together now!
DM

To Dave Morley, for friendship and inspiration.
RB

Contents

Foreword

There have been a number of effective books and articles over the years about the nature and development of physical education and sport but this latest book, based on the work of Dave Morley and Richard Bailey, pulls the essentials together with clarity and cogent reflection. It is certainly not solely a 'how to' book, nor a theoretical analysis, but succeeds powerfully in bringing the two together. It also manages to show very clearly that the gifted and talented agenda is entirely compatible with the demands for equity and social justice. Consequently for the teacher or the coordinator in schools, at the very heart of the book is a long-term commitment to *upskill* the teaching and *upgrade* the provision and understanding of PE and sport.

Starting with a useful analysis of how sport and PE play out differently (often with conflicting interests!) there are a number of enlightening perspectives that provide both commentary on and strategies for the harmonious interplay between the two. This is commendable, given the anecdotal comments of some of our elite (e.g. Sally Gunnell) that their talent may not have emerged without a strong school influence.

The authors have provided an outstanding contextual base for PE and sport, noting both theory and practical application. The book also serves to remind the reader that the role of pedagogy, in both areas, is frequently undervalued. There are some excellent observations and ideas on talent identification and the dangers of unrecognised talent remaining so. Reading this book provides a greater understanding of the scope and potential pathways in PE and sport.

The guidance in this book will be essential reading for PE G&T coordinators and teachers. It will provide a useful underpinning for the PE Quality Standards, which will be available simultaneously.

As a former PE teacher, sports obsessive and general educator, I found this book thought-provoking and highly informative.

PETER FROST

Gifted and Talented Education Unit, Department for Education and Skills

Foreword

This book presents a great opportunity to reflect upon and realign both thinking and practice in the education of gifted and talented pupils. As such, it will be useful not only to teachers but also to physical education advisers.

In a current climate that promotes an emphasis on gifted and talented provision in physical education and sport, supported by the Department for Education and Skill's (DfES) Physical Education, School Sport and Club Links strategy (PESSCL), this publication brings to the forefront the most up-to-date knowledge base in the areas of talent identification, provision, development and support in physical education. Some of the key principles and messages are also directly applicable to talented pupils who participate in sport within and/or outside of school and as such closes the circle or continuum from talent in physical education through to the world of sport.

The current national agenda on provision and support for talented pupils in physical education requires schools to adopt a more consistent and applied approach to gifted and talented education. This means whole-school policies and gifted and talented policies for physical education as a subject area, as well as provision and development of all abilities in physical education and sport over and above psychomotor performance. This emphasis on quality provision and support for talented pupils in physical education will help ensure that the government's Public Service Agreement (PSA) targets ensuring a minimum of 75 per cent of all pupils engage in high-quality physical education and sport by 2006, rising to 85 per cent of all pupils sustained in high quality involvement by 2008, are met.

I have no doubt that the longer term development and success of talented pupils in schools, and the impact of this success on pupil attainment and achievement, will be further enhanced by the knowledge that practitioners and advisers can gain from the content knowledge provided by the authors.

BEN TAN

National Manager (G&T Strand PESSCL), Youth Sport Trust

Foreword

It is inconceivable that a school can claim to be taking forward the personalisation agenda seriously without having a robust approach to gifted and talented education.

(Rt Hon. Jacqui Smith MP, Minister of State, Schools and
14–19 Learners, January 2006)

Effective schools provide an appropriate education for all pupils. They focus on the needs of individuals and design their offer to take account of the needs of the main recognised groups. Gifted and talented pupils are now a recognised group within each school. For a school to be effective it must plan its provision for these pupils, identify those who will benefit and monitor the effectiveness of their offer through its impact on the learning outcomes of pupils. This formalises the position of gifted and talented education and ensures that the needs of the most able are not overlooked.

Since 2000 we have begun to see the impact of a clear focus on the needs of gifted and talented pupils in the education system. The Qualifications and Curriculum Authority (QCA) and the National Strategies have begun to focus on this group and to provide materials and training to support teachers. The Office for Standards in Education (Ofsted) takes their needs into account when assessing the performance of a school and the government has established the National Academy for Gifted and Talented Youth (NAGTY) to steer this agenda.

NAGTY's role is to drive forward improvements in gifted and talented education by developing a national, government-supported catalyst that can provide leadership and support for professionals working in this field. To achieve this, it works with students, parents, teachers, education professionals, specialist providers, universities and business. Children and young people are at the heart of the Academy's mission. NAGTY aims to ensure that all children and young people, regardless of background, have access to the formal and informal learning opportunities they need to help them convert their potential into high achievement.

Gifted education in England is very much part of the overall education system and deeply embedded in it. The English model of gifted and talented education is a description of this approach and the rationale for it. Provision is rooted in day-to-day classroom provision and enhanced by additional, more advanced opportunities offered both within school and outside of it. Giftedness is a term used to describe children or adults who have the *capacity* to achieve high levels of expertise or performance. Giftedness in childhood could be described as 'expertise in its development phase'. Therefore, the education of gifted and talented pupils should focus on expertise development. Giftedness is developmental and is developed through individuals gaining access to appropriate opportunities and support. Performance levels are directly affected by availability of appropriate opportunities and support. Direct intervention with individuals can help reverse the effect of socioeconomic disadvantage or other lack of support.

Provision for gifted children should be made in ordinary schools as part of the day-to-day educational offer. This core provision should be supplemented by access to enhanced opportunities offered both within and beyond the school. Schools should themselves be diverse and distinctive in nature and so offer specific opportunities to develop certain aptitudes and parents should be seen as co-educators with a key role in supporting learning.

This series of books is a welcome addition to the literature base. It aims to help teachers make the English model a reality. In this model every teacher needs to be a teacher of the gifted. They need to understand how to teach the gifted and talented and have both the confidence and the skills to make that a reality on a day-to-day basis. While there are generic aspects to provision for gifted and talented pupils, the majority of classroom provision is subject-based and so it is through a subject approach that most teachers will consider the needs of their most able pupils. This series of books aims to help teachers within the subject domains to become more effective teachers of the gifted and talented pupils in their class. It builds on the emerging frameworks supplied by DfES, NAGTY and the government agencies and interprets them within a subject-specific context.

Without doubt this series of books will be a considerable help to both individual teachers and to schools seeking to improve provision for their gifted and talented children and young people.

PROFESSOR DEBORAH EYRE
Director, NAGTY

Acknowledgements

The contents of this book have been driven by research, training and development spanning the past five years. This process has involved numerous colleagues devoting their time to the search for a more informed understanding of talent development in PE and sport – to them we are eternally indebted.

Thanks to Crispin Andrews for his invaluable contributions to the style and fluency of the book and particularly for his thought-provoking and enlightening input into the Introduction and Chapter 6.

We would also like to thank Richard Tremere, Harriet Dismore, Paul Carney, Chris Carpenter, Ian Wellard, Steve Cobley, Graham Turner, Chris Buckley, Joanne Geoghan, Ray Godfrey, Claire Rotherham, Ben Mallinson, Trudy Fabian and Frances Bullimore for their tireless efforts on the 'Talent development in PE' project.

Thanks to the many schools and teachers from across the country for the invaluable contribution to this work. In a very literal sense, this book would not have been possible without them.

Thanks to Ben Tan, Andy Martin, Matt Smith and Kealey Sherwood from the Youth Sport Trust for their support with the project and the development of multi-skills.

Thanks to Jeanne Keay, Dave Haskins, Ian Pickup, Sue Cooper, Paul Moseley, Lyn Taylor, Andy Beddow, Tony Macfadyen and Dominic Haydn-Davies for their input on the development of quality standards for talent development in PE.

A final thank you to the Department for Education and Skills for funding the 'Talent development in PE' project and for their permission to use a selection of materials from the project within this book. The Gifted and Talented Sport programme is part of the government's national Physical Education, School Sport and Club Links strategy funded by the Departments for Education and Skills and for Culture, Media and Sport.

Contributors to the series

About the authors

David Morley has taught physical education in a number of secondary schools. He is currently senior lecturer in physical education at Leeds Metropolitan University and the director of the national DfES-funded 'Development in PE' project which is part of the Gifted and Talented strand of the PE, School Sport and Club Links (PESSCL) project. He is also a member of the team responsible for developing resources for national Multi-skill Clubs and is the founder and director of the Carnegie Regional Multi-skill Camp held at Leeds Met Carnegie.

Richard Bailey is a professor of pedagogy at Roehampton University, having previously worked at Reading and Leeds Metropolitan University, and at Canterbury Christ Church University where he was director of the Centre for Physical Education Research. He is a well-known author and speaker on physical education, sport and education.

Series editor

Gwen Goodhew's many and varied roles within the field of gifted and talented education have included school G&T coordinator, director of Wirral Able Children Centre, Knowsley Excellence in Cities (EiC) G&T coordinator, member of the DfES G&T Advisory Group, teacher trainer and consultant. She has written and edited numerous reports and articles on the subject and co-authored *Providing for Able Children* with Linda Evans.

Other authors

Art

Kim Earle is a former secondary head of art and design and is currently an able pupils and arts consultant for St Helens. She has been a member of DfES steering groups, is an Artsmark validator, a subject editor for G&TWISE and is a practising designer jeweller and enameller.

Design and Technology

During the writing of the book **Louise T. Davies** was a part-time subject adviser for design and technology at the QCA (Qualifications and Curriculum Authority), and part of the KS3 National Strategy team for the D&T programme. She has authored over 40 D&T books and award-winning multimedia resources. She is currently deputy chief executive of the Design and Technology Association.

Music

Jonathan Savage is a senior lecturer in music education at the Institute of Education, Manchester Metropolitan University. Until 2001 he was head of music at Debenham High School, an 11–16 comprehensive school in Suffolk. He is a co-author of a new resource introducing computer game sound design to the Key Stage 3 curriculum (www.sound2game.net) and managing director of UCan.tv (www.ucan.tv), a company specialising in the production of educational software and hardware. When not doing all of this, he is busy parenting four very musically talented children!

Contents of the CD

The CD accompanying this book may be used by the purchasing individual/organisation only. It contains files which may be amended to suit particular situations, or individual learning needs, and printed out for use by the purchaser.

Highlights from the CD

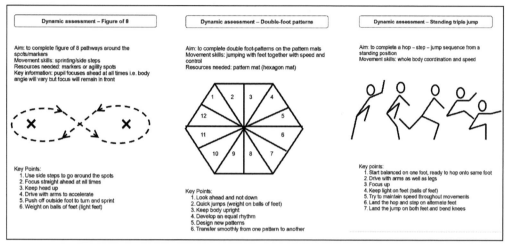

Three of the 13 dynamic assessment exercises

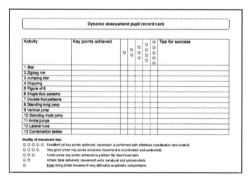

The dynamic assessment pupil record card

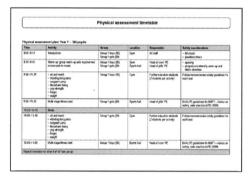

A timetable for a physical assessment morning

The 'Identifying Creativity in Dance' short-term plan

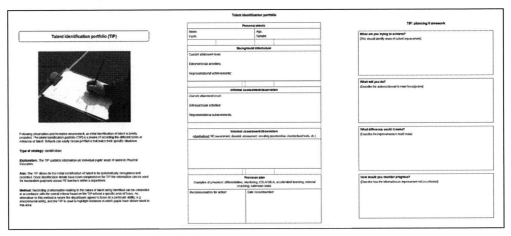

The talent identification portfolion (TIP)

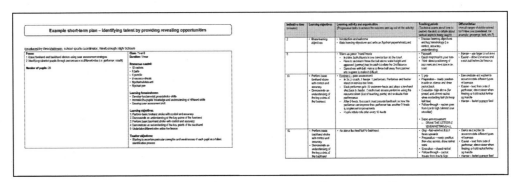

A sample short-term plan for identifying talent by providing revealing opportunities

From the 'revealing opportunities' short-term plan

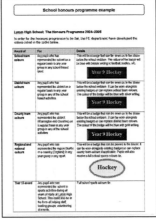

A sample school honours programme

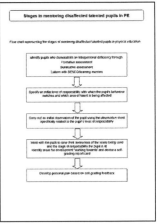

The stages in mentoring disaffected talented pupils in PE

Introduction

Who should use this book?

This book is for all teachers of physical education working with Key Stage 3 and Key Stage 4 pupils. It will be relevant to teachers working within the full spectrum of schools, from highly selective establishments to comprehensive and secondary modern schools as well as some special schools. Its overall objective is to provide a practical resource that heads of department, gifted and talented coordinators and classroom teachers can use to develop a coherent approach to provision for their most able pupils.

Why is it needed?

School populations differ greatly and pupils considered very able in one setting might not stand out in another. Nevertheless, whatever the general level of ability within a school, there has been a tendency to plan and provide for the middle range, to modify for those who are struggling and to leave the most able to 'get on with it'. This has meant that the most able have:

- not been sufficiently challenged and stimulated

- often underachieved

- been unaware of what they might be capable of achieving

- not had high enough ambitions and aspirations

- sometimes become disaffected.

For those involved in PE, the crossover into the world of sport brings with it another array of subject-specific issues that require consideration. It is not an overstatement to suggest that sport in this country is huge – it generates its own vast army of active and passive participants, and has its own media coverage, its own financial and business infrastructure and its own culture. Everyone, be they players, coaches, ground staff, administrators, volunteers or fans, will have their own opinions, ideas and vested interests. The beauty of sport, like education, is that these opinions, interests and ideas will inevitably differ and often clash.

This is the world within which teachers charged with meeting the specific needs of gifted and talented children in PE and sport must operate: a world where views generated by involvement in and passion for adult sport can sometimes determine attitudes towards sporting provision which may be pursuing quite different outcomes; a place where the often-conflicting self-interest of school, club, district, county and beyond can cloud the fact that, however good he or she is, it might not be in a youngster's best interests to play one sport so often at such an early age. It is also a world in which social and economic difficulties can create barriers to, but at the same time open up possibilities for, the development of a talented player. Today, practitioners must deliver programmes to get the best out of talented youngsters who display a multitude of different abilities within the boundaries of wider provision designed to meet the needs of all students. They must provide high quality competitive opportunities whilst at the same time designing projects that have an effect beyond PE and sport, indeed beyond the school itself. Furthermore, they must do all this in settings where PE and sport may or may not have a high profile and irrespective of the quality of links with the local sporting community.

How will this book help teachers?

This book and its accompanying CD, through its combination of practical ideas, materials for photocopying or downloading, and case studies of individual pupils, departmental policy and practice, will:

- help teachers of physical education to focus on the top 5–10% of the ability range in their particular school and to find ways of providing for these pupils, both within and beyond the classroom

- equip them with strategies and ideas to support exceptionally able pupils, i.e. those in the top 5% nationally.

Terminology

Since there is confusion about the meaning of the words 'gifted' and 'talented', the terms 'more able', 'most able' and 'exceptionally able' will generally be used in this series.

When 'gifted' and 'talented' are used, the definitions provided by the Department for Education and Skills (DfES) in its Excellence in Cities programme will apply. That is:

- **gifted** pupils are the most academically able in a school. This ability might be general or specific to a particular subject area, such as mathematics.

- **talented** pupils are those with high ability or potential in art, music, performing arts, physical education or sport.

The two groups together should form 5–10% of any school population.

There are, of course, some pupils who are both gifted and talented. Examples that come to mind are the budding physicist who plays the violin to a high standard in his spare time, or the pupil with high general academic ability who plays for the area football team.

This book is part of a series dealing with providing challenge for the most able secondary age pupils in a range of subjects. It is likely that some of the books in the series might also contain ideas that would be relevant to teachers of physical education.

CHAPTER 1

Our more able pupils – the national scene

The purpose of this first chapter is to place the subject-specific content of all that follows into the more general national and school framework. We know it is easier to understand what needs to be done at departmental level if there is an appreciation of the context in which discussions are held and decisions are made.

The debate about whether to make special provision for the most able pupils in secondary schools ran its course during the last decade of the twentieth century. Explicit provision to meet their learning needs is now considered neither elitist nor a luxury. From an inclusion angle, these pupils must have the same chances as others to develop their potential to the full. We know from international research that focusing on the needs of the most able changes teachers' perceptions of the needs of all their pupils, and there follows a consequential rise in standards. But for teachers who are not convinced by the inclusion or school improvement arguments, there is a much more pragmatic reason for meeting the needs of able pupils. Of course, it is preferable that colleagues share a common willingness to address the needs of the most able, but if they do not, it can at least be pointed out that, quite simply, it is something that all teachers are now required to do, not an optional extra.

> All schools should seek to create an atmosphere in which to excel is not only acceptable but desirable.
>
> (*Excellence in Schools* – DfEE 1997)

> High achievement is determined by the school's commitment to inclusion and the steps it takes to ensure that every pupil does as well as possible.
>
> (*Handbook for Inspecting Secondary Schools* – Ofsted 2003)

A few years ago, efforts to raise standards in schools concentrated on getting as many pupils as possible over the Level 5 hurdle at the end of Key Stage 3 and over the five A*–C grades hurdle at GCSE. Resources were pumped into borderline pupils and the most able were not, on the whole, considered a cause for concern. The situation has changed dramatically in the last five years with schools being expected to set targets for A*s and As and to show added value by helping pupils entering the school with high SATs scores to achieve Levels 7 and beyond, if supporting data suggests that that is what is achievable. Early recognition of high potential and the setting of curricular targets are at last addressing the lack of progress demonstrated by many able pupils in Year 7 and more attention is being paid to creating a climate in which learning can flourish. Nevertheless, there is a push for even more support for the most able through the promotion of personalised learning.

> The goal is that five years from now: gifted and talented students progress in line with their ability rather than their age; schools inform parents about tailored provision in an annual school profile; curricula include a gifted and talented dimension and at 14–19 there is more stretch and differentiation at the top-end, so no matter what your talent it will be engaged; and the effect of poverty on achievement is reduced, because support for high-ability students from poorer backgrounds enables them to thrive.
>
> (Speech at the National Academy for Gifted and Talented Youth – David Miliband, Minister for State for School Standards, May 2004)

It is hoped that this book, with the others in this series, will help to accelerate these changes.

Making good provision for the most able – what's in it for schools?

Schools and/or subject departments often approach provision for the most able pupils with some reluctance because they imagine a lot of extra work for very little reward. In fact, the rewards of providing for these pupils are substantial:

● It can be very stimulating to the subject specialist to explore ways of developing approaches with enthusiastic and able students.

> Taking a serious look at what I should expect from the most able and then at how I should teach them has given my teaching a new lease of life. I feel so sorry for youngsters who were taught by me 10 years ago. They must have been bored beyond belief. But then, to be quite honest, so was I.
>
> (science teacher)

● Offering opportunities to tackle work in a more challenging manner often interests pupils whose abilities have gone unnoticed because they have not been motivated by a bland educational diet.

> Some of the others were invited to an after-school maths club. When I heard what they were doing, it sounded so interesting that I asked the maths teacher if I could go too. She was a bit doubtful at first because I have messed about a lot but she agreed to take me on trial. I'm one of her star pupils now and she reckons I'll easily get an A*. I still find some of

the lessons really slow and boring but I don't mess around – well, not too much.

(Year 10 boy)

- When pupils are engaged by the work they are doing, motivation, attainment and discipline improve.

  You don't need to be gifted to work out that the work we do is much more interesting and exciting. It's made others want to be like us.
  (Comment from a student involved in an extension programme for the most able)

- Schools that are identified as very good schools by Ofsted generally have good provision for their most able students.

  If you are willing to deal effectively with the needs of able pupils you will raise the achievement of all pupils.
  (Mike Tomlinson, former director of Ofsted)

- The same is true of individual departments in secondary schools. All those considered to be very good have spent time developing a sound working approach that meets the needs of their most able pupils.

  The department creates a positive atmosphere by its organisation, display and the way that students are valued. Learning is generally very good and often excellent throughout the school. The teachers' high expectations permeate the atmosphere and are a significant factor in raising achievement. These expectations are reflected in the curriculum which has depth and students are able and expected to experience difficult problems in all year groups.
  (Mathematics department, Hamstead Hall School, Birmingham, Ofsted 2003)

National initiatives since 1997

Since 1997, when the then Department for Education and Employment (DfEE) set up its Gifted and Talented Advisory Group, many initiatives designed to raise aspirations and levels of achievement have been targeted on the most able, especially in secondary schools. Currently, a three-pronged approach is in place, with:

1. special programmes, including Excellence in Cities, Excellence Clusters and Aimhigher, for areas of the country where educational standards in secondary schools are lowest

2. resources for teachers and pupils throughout the country, such as the National Academy for Gifted and Talented Youth, gifted and talented summer schools, World Class Tests, National Curriculum Online and the G&TWISE website

3. regional support, which is currently confined to GATE A, in London.

1. Special programmes

Excellence in Cities

In an attempt to deal with the chronic underachievement of able pupils in inner city areas, Excellence in Cities (EiC) was launched in 1999. This is a very ambitious, well-funded programme with many different strands. It initially concentrated on secondary age pupils but work has been extended into the primary sector in many areas. 'Provision for the Gifted and Talented' is one of the strands.

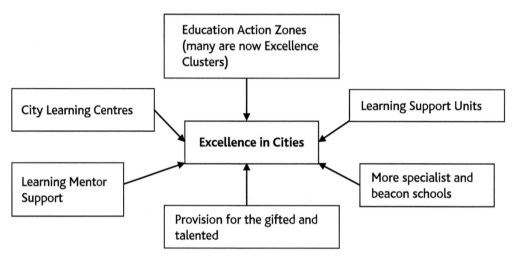

Strands in the Excellence in Cities initiative

EiC schools are expected to:

- develop a whole-school policy for their most able pupils

- appoint a gifted and talented coordinator with sufficient time to fulfil the role

- send the coordinator on a national training programme run by Oxford Brookes University

- identify 5–10% of pupils in each year group as their gifted and talented cohort, the gifted being the academically able and the talented being those with latent or obvious ability in PE, sport, music, art or the performing arts

- provide an appropriate programme of work both within the school day and beyond

- set 'aspirational' targets both for the gifted and talented cohort and for individual pupils

- work with other schools in a 'cluster' to provide further support for these pupils

- work with other agencies, such as Aimhigher, universities, businesses and private-sector schools, to enhance provision and opportunities for these pupils.

The influence of Excellence in Cities has stretched far beyond the areas where it is in place. There are a number of reasons for this:

- Partnership (LEA) gifted and talented coordinators set up regional support groups. These groups worked to raise awareness of the needs of these pupils and their teachers. One of the most successful is the Transpennine Group, which operates from Liverpool across to Hull. Early meetings concentrated on interpreting Department for Education and Skills (DfES) directives but later the group invited universities, support organisations, publishers and successful practitioners to share ideas with them. They also began to run activities for pupils across all the EiC partnerships involved. By constantly feeding back information from the meetings to the DfES, it began to have some influence on policy. Teachers and advisers outside EiC areas have adopted similar models and the DfES is now funding regional support groups that include both EiC and non-EiC areas.

- Publishers have responded to demand from gifted and talented coordinators and are producing more materials, both books and software, that challenge the most able.

- Some LEAs have worked with Oxford Brookes University to extend their coordinator training into non-EiC areas.

- **The requirements of EiC schools have come to be regarded as a blueprint for all secondary schools.** The DfES guidance for EiC schools is available for all schools at www.standards.dfes.gov.uk/giftedandtalented.

Excellence Clusters

Although EiC was set up initially in the main urban conurbations, other hotspots of underachievement and poverty have since been identified and Excellence Clusters have been established. For example, Ellesmere Port, Crewe and Barrow-in-Furness are pockets of deprivation, with major social problems and significant underachievement, in otherwise affluent areas. Excellence Clusters have been established in these three places and measures are being taken to improve provision for the most able pupils.

Aimhigher

There have been a number of changes in EiC over the years. One of the most recent is that, in secondary schools, the EiC programme now supports the most able between the ages of 11 and 14, but from 14 to 19 their needs are met through Aimhigher, another initiative of the DfES. Its remit is to widen participation in UK higher education, particularly among students from groups that do not have a tradition of going to university, such as ethnic minorities, the disabled and those from poorer homes. Support for these pupils begins while they are still in school and includes:

- activities in schools and colleges to encourage them and raise their aspirations

- extra money to universities to enable them to provide summer schools and outreach work with pupils

- The Young People's Publicity Campaign providing information and advice to those from disadvantaged backgrounds

- financial support for students through 26,000 Opportunity Bursaries worth £2,000 each over three years for young people.

The Aimhigher website is at www.aimhigher.ac.uk.

Physical Education, School Sport and Club Links (PESSCL)

The PESSCL strategy was launched in October 2002 and is run jointly by the Department for Education and Skills (DfES) and the Department for Culture, Media and Sport (DCMS). PESSCL is associated with a committed investment of £1 billion, primarily delivered through the network of sports colleges and school sport partnerships (DfES, 2003). The initial overall objective was to ensure that by 2006, 75 per cent of 5- to 16-year-olds in England are spending a minimum of two hours each week on high quality PE and school sport, within and beyond the curriculum. By 2008, the target is that 85 per cent of pupils will experience two hours of PE each week.

It is hoped that this will be achieved through the delivery of eight programmes, each of which is aimed at contributing towards achieving the overall objective. The eight programme areas are:

- specialist sports colleges

- school sport coordinator programme

- national professional development programme

- swimming

- coaching

- 'Step into Sport'

- school to club links

- gifted and talented programme

An integral part of the strategy is the infrastructure built around the sports college and school sport partnerships, each of which is made up of a family of schools who work in partnership to increase and enhance sport and physical activity opportunities for all pupils. An average partnership is made up of a sports college, acting as the hub, about eight secondary schools and about 40 primary schools clustered around the sports college and secondary schools.

Each school sport partnership receives a grant to deliver this work. A key part of this funding is the provision of a full-time partnership development manager (PDM) for each partnership. This person is solely dedicated to managing and developing the programme. In many areas, secondary schools also have a school sport coordinator, who is released from teaching for part of a week to support the PDM on programmes and initiatives to meet the targets identified below:

1. raise standards of pupils' achievement in all aspects of school life

2. provide training and leadership opportunities for pupils, teachers and adults other than teachers

3. improve PE and school sport programmes by establishing and developing links between schools, especially around the Key Stage 2/3 interface

4. provide and enhance out-of-school-hours learning opportunities in PE and school sport

5. increase participation of young people in community sport through creating and strengthening partnerships with community providers

6. develop and implement a partnership strategy aimed at meeting the government target.

Like EiC, PESSCL includes a distinct gifted and talented strand, dedicated to improving the range and quality of teaching, coaching and learning for pupils talented in sports in order to raise their attainment, aspirations, motivation and self-esteem. Nationally, the strand, which is being delivered by schools and national governing bodies of sport, includes:

- a talent support programme for school sport partnerships with support from a national faculty of trainers

- local multi-skill academies to help identify potentially talented young performers

- national performance camps for elite athletes, organised by national governing bodies

- pilot development programmes to coordinate a multi-agency approach to talent development in local communities

- web-based resources for teachers, coaches and parents

- advice, guidance and training for teachers of talented pupils in PE, as part of the National Curriculum

- a disability sport coordinator to develop support for talented disabled athletes, ensuring that the remainder of the project takes account of their needs

- support for research in the development of talented children, and access to it for teachers and coaches

- a school-based profiling and tracking system.

2. Resources for teachers and pupils throughout the country

Recent developments in gifted and talented education within PE and sport have been associated with the appearance of a series of useful programmes and initiatives designed to support schools and teachers. Many of these have been brought under the umbrella of the PESSCL strategy, but each has its own focus and value. Some of the most relevant for schools and teachers are listed below.

Junior Athlete Education programme

www.talentladder.org/tl_supp.html

The Junior Athlete Education programme (JAE) is coordinated by the Youth Sport Trust at Loughborough University, and forms a common feature of the national talent development programme. It is designed to offer a comprehensive range of support materials and processes for talented young sports people. The programme is supported by national governing bodies for sport, and is implemented through specialist sports colleges and their partner secondary and primary schools. So, it reflects the consensus view that talent development in sport is likely to prove most effective when schools and sports groups work together, within a system of shared practices and goals.

Multi-skills academies

www.talentladder.org/tl_msc.html

Multi-skills academies for gifted and talented pupils reflect current conceptions of best practice, since they are premised upon offering talented pupils in physical education and sport a broad foundation of practical, generic skills, underpinned by sound theoretical knowledge. There has been a danger in the past of focusing too narrowly upon a single sporting or physical activity, which research has shown to be ineffective in the long term in maintaining motivation and developing talent, and can be potentially harmful for children's development. The multi-skills academy project, which is located within the PESSCL programme, offers a framework for talent identification and provision that includes both physical and non-physical abilities. It can, therefore, be seen as a compliment to the multi-ability approach advocated in this book.

Quality Standards for Physical Education

www.youthsporttrust.org/talentladder/tl_supp_curr.html

The Quality Standards for Physical Education provide the most comprehensive guidance available for the identification of and provision for talented pupils in physical education and sport. The Quality Standards provide a series of statements of outcome that reflect different degrees of good practice, from requisite (or basic) to exemplary. These statements are supplemented by strategies and tools that can help local authorities and schools progress towards exemplary practice. The Quality Standards are organised around six central themes: policy, professional development, identification and selection, teaching and provision, supporting talented pupils, and managing talent in physical education, and are differentiated to support development at different levels, including local education authorities, schools, parents and pupils. This framework will allow different groups the opportunity to select the materials that are of greatest relevance to their needs, and suggest practical approaches to ensure ongoing improvement.

Talent Matters

www.talentmatters.org

Talent Matters is currently the only UK site dedicated to supporting the teaching of talented pupils in physical education (rather than sport or education in general). Although it is a relatively new development, and some parts are still under construction, this is an outstanding resource for LEAs, schools, parents and teachers of talented pupils, and provides a great amount of valuable material and advice. Linked to a large-scale national research project within the government's Physical Education, School Sport and Club Links (PESSCL) scheme, and written by the authors of the Quality Standards for Talent Development for Physical Education (www.talentmatters.org/qs01/qs.htm), the site offers a sophisticated, yet practical approach to meeting the needs of very able pupils, based on the most recent guidance and conceptions of best practice.

Talent Ladder

www.talentladder.org

The Talent Ladder website is a key part of the PESSCL strategy aiming to provide a communication tool and central resource area to all individuals involved with young people who are G&T in PE and sport, be they the young people themselves, their teachers, parents/guardians or their coaches. The support for G&T section contains information, guidance and resources devoted to the talent support programme, Junior Athlete Education (see above), as well as talent development in curriculum PE and its associated research. The multi-skill clubs and performance camps sections provide information and reports on the more practical side of G&T in the national framework for PE and sport in PESSCL. Research in G&T is a section that aims to provide information about talent identification and development research findings that are being generated from the academic community. And, finally, in the disability G&T section, information is available regarding current project work being carried out to support school sport partnerships to identify and provide for G&T pupils with a disability.

National Curriculum for Physical Education

www.nc.uk.net

The value of the site is probably self-evident. However, it is always worth remembering that the progressive nature of the PE curriculum means that it will always be of relevance in discussions of talent development, and the Exceptional Performance level descriptions can substantiate any talent identification.

The Standards Site

www.standards.dfes.gov.uk

A logical next step after reading the National Curriculum guidance is to consider the DfES/QCA's schemes of work. The different themes (based on PE's areas of activity) are comprehensive, and include some valuable guidance on extending and enriching children's learning that could be understood as talent development by another name.

Physical Education, School Sport and Club Links National Strategy homepage

www.teachernet.gov.uk/teachingandlearning/subjects/pe

This site contains news and updates on the national PESSCL strategy. Its main function seems to be to act as a portal for the government's guidance, press releases and publications. So, this is a useful place to search for specific information on policy and statutory requirements for talent development in PE.

National Academy for Gifted and Talented Youth

Government initiatives for the most able pupils have not been confined to those in deprived areas. In 2002, the National Academy for Gifted and Talented Youth was established at Warwick University. Its brief is to offer support to the most able 5% of the school population and to their teachers and parents, and it is doing this in a number of ways.

The National Academy for Gifted and Talented Youth		
Student Academy	**Professional Academy**	**Expertise Centre**
• Summer schools, including link-ups with the Center for Talented Youth (CTY) in the USA • Outreach courses in a wide range of subjects at universities and other venues across the country • Online activities – currently maths, classics, ethics and philosophy	• Continuing professional development (CPD) for teachers • A PGCE+ programme for trainee teachers • Ambassador School Programme to disseminate good practice amongst schools	• Leading research in gifted and talented education

Bursaries are available for pupils from low-income families so that they are not denied access to the activities. The Academy's website is at www.nagty.ac.uk.

Gifted and talented summer schools

Each LEA is provided with money to run a number of summer schools (dependent on the size of the authority) for the most able pupils in Years 6–9. The approach to the selection and management of these schools differs from area to area. For example, some authorities organise them centrally while others allow schools to bid to run one of the summer schools. The main aim obviously is to challenge and stimulate these pupils but the DfES also hopes that:

- the summer schools will encourage teachers and advisers to adopt innovative teaching approaches

- teachers will continue to monitor these pupils over time

- where Year 6 pupils are involved, it will make secondary teachers aware of what they can achieve and raise their expectations of Year 7 pupils.

More can be found out about these summer schools at: www.standards.dfes.gov.uk/giftedandtalented/. Unfortunately, direct funding from the DfES for summer schools ceased in 2005.

World Class Tests

These have been introduced by the Qualifications and Curriculum Authority (QCA) to allow schools to judge the performance of their most able pupils against national and international standards. Tests are currently available for 9- and 13-year-olds in mathematics and problem solving. Some schools have found that the problem solving tests are effective at identifying able underachievers in maths and science. The website, at www.worldclassarena.org.uk, contains sample questions so that teachers, parents and pupils themselves can assess the tests' suitability for particular pupils or groups of pupils.

National Curriculum Online

The National Curriculum Online website, administered by QCA, provides general guidance on all aspects of the National Curriculum but also has a substantial section on general and subject-specific issues relating to gifted and talented education, including identification strategies, case studies, management and units of work. The website is at www.nc.uk.net/gt.

G&TWISE

The G&TWISE website has recently replaced the one called Xcalibre. It links to recommended resources for gifted and talented pupils, checked by professionally qualified subject editors, in all subjects and at all Key Stages. It is part-funded by the Gifted and Talented Education Unit of the DfES. The website is at www2.teachernet.gov.uk/gat/.

3. Regional support

At this stage, regional support is confined to GATE A, a branch of London Challenge. Four London EiC partnerships have collaborated with universities, cultural centres and professional bodies to develop a coordinated approach to supporting the most able pupils throughout the region.

Central to this is the MLE or Managed Learning Environment, which provides pupils with interactive learning materials. Some key feature of this include:

- videoconferencing and online alerts for specific groups of users

- online assignments and tests

- course calendars and linked personal calendars

- personal study records.

GATE A provides five 'Student Learning Pathways' so that the approach can be matched to a student's stage of development and needs. There are subject, themed and cross-curricular skills-based pathways as well as one directed at Aimhigher students, and one for work-related learning. The initiative also strives to support the parents and carers of more able pupils. The website is at www.londongt.org.

The initiatives discussed above do not include the many subject-specific developments, such as those from QCA, that have taken place during this period. These will be dealt with in later chapters.

LEA responsibilities to more able pupils

Schools and departments should not be shy of approaching their LEA for help when developing their more able pupil provision. Local authorities, as well as schools, are expected to support more able pupils and schools can and should turn to them for support and advice.

The notes from Ofsted on LEA Link Inspection published in December 2003 state that the main tasks of LEAs, with regard to offering support to schools for gifted and talented pupils, are:

- to provide guidance to schools in meeting pupils' needs

- to identify schools which need particular help and to ensure that this is provided effectively

- where appropriate, to support initiatives across the LEA, such as gifted and talented summer schools, Excellence in Cities, Excellence Clusters and helping pupils to access resources such as the National Academy for Gifted and Talented Youth

- to support individual pupils with particular talents in order that they make progress

- to learn lessons from Excellence in Cities areas.

After a period when many LEAs did very little to support these pupils in a systematic manner, the climate has now changed and many have taken measures such as:

- producing gifted and talented guidelines for schools

- running continuing professional development (CPD) programmes, sometimes with the help of Oxford Brookes University, which provide training for EiC gifted and talented coordinators

- encouraging federations of local schools to work together to make additional provision for the most able

- setting up masterclasses and advanced learning centres

- identifying good practice in schools and disseminating this to other schools in the authority.

Ofsted – expectations of secondary schools

The most able must be seen to have as many opportunities for development as other pupils. Poor, unchallenging teaching or an ideology that confuses equality of opportunity with levelling down must not hinder their progress. The environment for learning should be one in which it is safe to be clever or to excel.

Throughout the new Ofsted *Handbook for Inspecting Secondary Schools* (2003), there are both direct and indirect references to schools' responsibilities to their most able pupils. Wherever the phrase 'all pupils should . . .' appears in this handbook, teachers need to ask themselves not only how this applies to pupils with special educational needs (SEN) and other disadvantaged groups but also how this applies to their most able pupils.

A summary of some of the more important points relating to more able pupils from this handbook is included in Appendix 1.1, where page numbers are provided so that teachers can find out more.

Some tools to support inspection and school development plans

In light of the above, teachers might find the Pre-Ofsted checklist overleaf and the National Quality Standards in Gifted and Talented Education (Appendix 1.2) helpful either when preparing for Ofsted or when looking into developing this area of work as part of the school development plan. More about national quality standards in gifted and talented education can be found at www.standards.dfes.gov.uk/ giftedandtalented/strategyandstrands.

It is important to remember that:

- the development of provision for the more able should be firmly enmeshed with other curricular and pastoral strategies and should fit in to the overall school philosophy

- classroom practice should match school and departmental policy.

	Pre-Ofsted able pupil checklist	✓
1.	Does the school have a policy for its most able pupils?	
2.	Is there a school coordinator for the most able?	
3.	Is there someone in each department with whom the coordinator can liaise?	
4.	Are there identification strategies in place that are understood by all?	
5.	Do these strategies identify both academic ability and talent in specific areas of the curriculum?	
6.	Does the balance of the most able cohort match the school profile in terms of gender, ethnicity and social class?	
7.	Do pupils' achievements match their potential taking into account the school's performance data and other evidence?	
8.	Is negative stereotyping of the most able challenged?	
9.	Do teachers support the most able with: – high expectations?	
10.	– the employment of a wide range of teaching styles?	
11.	– a suitable pace?	
12.	– extension and enrichment activities?	
13.	– the selection of suitable resources?	
14.	Does the school's organisation of pupils into groups and sets take account of the needs of these pupils?	
15.	Does the school have an appropriate curriculum for the most able?	
16.	Do pupils have access to any of the following: learning mentors; study support; out-of-school activities; masterclasses; specialists; resources in other schools and colleges?	
17.	Are senior managers alert to the need to monitor and track the progress of the most able?	
18.	Is suitable training for staff arranged when the need arises?	
19.	Do senior managers take action when the needs of the most able are not being met?	
20.	Are the most able pupils positive about the education and support they receive in the school?	
21.	Are parents content with school provision?	

Other general support for teachers and parents of more able pupils

Two organisations which must be included when there is any mention of support for more able pupils, their teachers and parents are NACE and NAGC.

NACE

The National Association for Able Children in Education, or NACE as it is generally known, is primarily a support organisation for teaching professionals. It has many publications on the education of more able pupils, many of them produced in association with David Fulton Publishers. Its Challenge Award has been particularly well received. Conferences are regularly held around the country and training can be provided at school, LEA or regional level. It can also provide consultancy tailored to the individual needs of schools. The Association's website is at www.nace.co.uk.

NAGC

The focus of the National Association for Gifted Children is primarily on the children themselves although it does offer support to parents and teachers as well. It can offer:

- branches throughout the country where children with similar interests or abilities can meet at regular intervals

- online activities for 3- to 10-year-olds

- counselling for young people and parents

- support through its Youth Agency for 11- to 20-year-olds with web pages to which they have exclusive access

- INSET

- publications.

The Association's website is at www.nagcbritain.org.uk.

Talent development in PE and sport – the international picture

International models of talent development

It is difficult to discuss international developments in the same detail as those in the UK. Very few countries have explicitly considered talent development in physical education, and in most cases, the emphasis is on either 'gifted and talented education' for so-called 'academic' subjects or 'talent development in sport'. Either way, physical education, as a curriculum subject, is largely overlooked as the focus of enquiry.

This does not mean that physical education is not mentioned, at all, but that it is usually understood as part of a 'bigger picture'. For example, many sports development models from around the world do contain physical education as a key element, just not as the main point of the activity. So, we often see models such as the one overleaf.

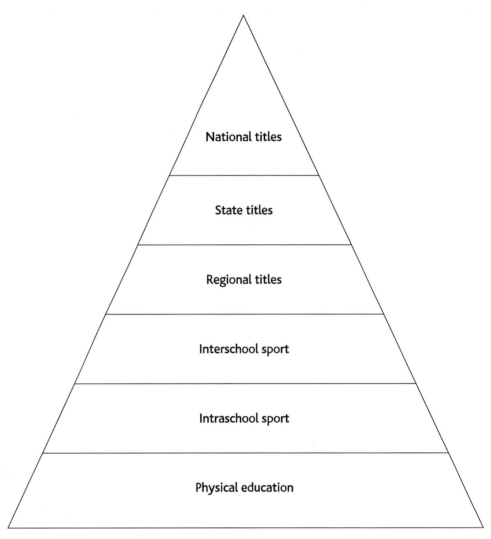

A pyramid model of the relationship between physical education and sport performance
(from Tinning *et al.*, 1993)

Diagrams like this reflect the very common assumption that physical education can act as the foundation of later sports performance, with increasingly high levels of performance engaged in by decreasing numbers of people. Whether it can or not is less clear. It does certainly seem to be the case that basic movement skills, like those developed in physical education, form the foundation of almost all later sporting and physical activities (Gallahue and Ozmun, 1998). But there have been very few (if any) studies that actually test this well-worn claim (Abbott *et al.*, 2002).

There are other, more fundamental, potential difficulties with the traditional sports development model, too. Kirk and Gorely (2000) offer some points by way of warning:

- if children are taught poorly at the base, we will be left with a large number of poor performers

- built into the pyramid's design is the systematic exclusion of young people, no matter how good they are, as fewer and fewer players can play at each level

- the pyramid is built on the dubious assumption that there really are clearly distinguishable levels of performers; in practice, things are not so simple.

Despite these problems, pyramid models of sports and talent development dominate national and international frameworks.

Sport England's current presentation of the relationship between physical education and sport clearly reflects the traditional model outlined above (see Sport England's current model of junior sport participation, illustrated below). According to this approach, the main role of schools (and especially physical education) is to act as the foundation of young people's sports participation by developing the basic knowledge, skills and understanding in a range of activities.

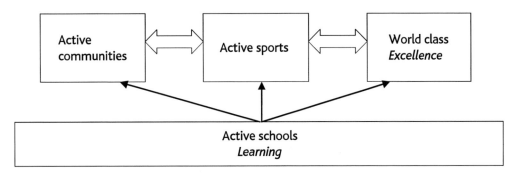

Sport England's current model of junior sport participation

Germany has developed a different approach, and many schools contribute to the country's talent development scheme. For example, talent identification and selection takes place in schools, and sports groups work with teachers to analyse performance in sports competitions and physical ability tests. Also, as in England, the country has seen the development of specialist sports schools, although these have a different character and intent.

German sports schools are designed specifically to support the education and sporting development of talented young people through opportunities to board at the school, as well as flexible timetabling of lessons and formal tests, to make it as easy as possible for these young players to succeed both within school and in their chosen sports.

Distinctive elements within the German specialist school model are:

- lessons are organised to allow sports training twice a day
- school examinations are coordinated with the training schedule and competition calendar
- remedial school lessons are available following sports training courses
- admission to university can be delayed
- specialist teachers are available at the boarding schools, to support the young sports people. (Kirk, Brettschneider and Auld, 2003).

A third country worth considering is New Zealand. With its small population, New Zealand does not have the benefit of large groups of potential players to bolster its teams, so it seems that educational and sporting groups have been forced to think very carefully about the development of talented young players. The system is based on close collaboration between sports clubs and schools, and explicitly basing talent development on general participation and recreation. 'The New Zealand model' below offers a simple representation of the ways in which schools work alongside other areas of sports participation, to help nurture and develop talent among New Zealand's young people.

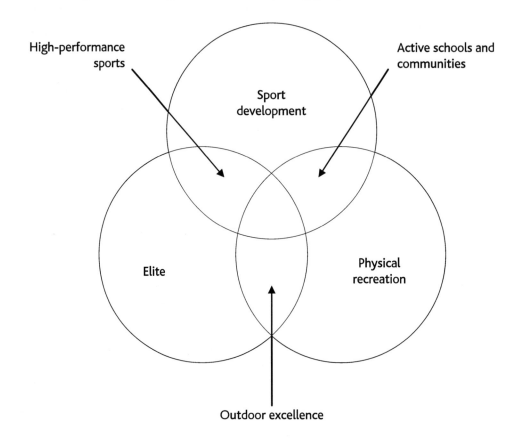

The New Zealand model (based on Kirk *et al.*, 2003)

Developmental models of sports talent development

As well as sports talent development models from different countries, it is worthwhile considering two other models. Each has proved influential in terms of encouraging national sports groups to construct their talent development programmes around the changing physical, emotional, intellectual and social makeup of young people. In short, both have stressed, as their central message, the vital importance of recognising children and not mini-adults, and that their development should inform any sensible talent development strategy. The first approach, called long-term athlete development (LTAD), was developed by Istvan Balyi. The second is based on the work of Jean Côté and John Hay. Coincidentally, both models originate in Canada.

Balyi's LTAD is based on findings from research in a number of areas that one of the most important ingredients of elite performance is practice (Starkes and

Ericsson, 2003). Consequently, he constructed a framework that aimed to progressively develop talent over a period of years (Balyi, 2001; Balyi and Hamilton, 2000). Balyi distinguishes between early and late specialisation sports. Early specialisation sports are those that involve competition and training at a relatively young age, such as gymnastics, figure skating and diving. Later specialisation sports, which account for the great majority of activities, require a more generalised approach to early training. Although there are some differences between these two sets of activities, the most relevant stages are essentially the same (in the model for early specialisation, the first top stages are combined), and are outlined in the table below.

Key features of Balyi's LTAD model (based on Balyi and Hamilton, 2000)

Stage	Age	Key features
FUNdamental	Male: 6–9 years Female: 6–8 years	• Structured and fun • Emphasis on fundamental movement skills, and agility, balance, coordination and speed • Use of games to develop skills • Children encouraged to play a number of games, and play throughout the week
Learning to train	Male: 9–12 years Female: 8–11 years	• Learning all fundamental movement skills • Building overall sports skills • Basic strength development – body weight, bounding, ball activities, etc. • Introducing basic flexibility and speed exercises • Well-structured competitions
Training to train	Male: 12–16 years Female: 11–15 years	• Building aerobic base and strength • Learning how to train • Learning basic skills of a specific sport, and the basic technical/tactical skills • Competitions are important, but the emphasis is on learning, not competing
Training to compete	Male: 16–18 years Female: 15–17 years	• Greater emphasis on competition • High-intensity sport-specific training • Special attention is given to individual preparation in terms of fitness and psychological training, and technical development
Training to win	Male: 18 years and older Female: 17 years and older	• Focus of training shifts to the optimisation of performance • High intensity and high volume training • Strong emphasis on training for competition

Balyi's model was informed by his work with regional and national sports groups. Côté and Hay's approach (2002), on the other hand, derives from a study of scientific research. Reviewing the academic literature, they concluded that young people's development in sport follows a general pattern, which can be represented as a simple diagram.

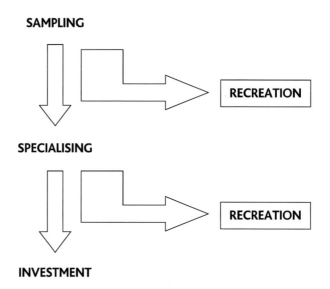

Graphical representation of Côté and Hay's model of young people's socialisation into sport

The 'sampling phase', which usually occurs between the ages of 8 and 14, is characterised by engagement in a wide range of sports. The main motivation for young people at this stage is enjoyment, and the emphasis is much more on playing than on training or competing. Côté and Hay talk about 'deliberate play', which means structured activities that require the development of technical and tactical competence.

Young people have three options as they approach their teenage years: they can carry on sampling sports, or they can switch to more informal and recreational play, or they can move on to play sport more seriously. This second phase is called the 'specialising phase', and usually occurs around 14 years of age. The number of sports played reduces, normally to one or two, and the focus of engagement changes from fun to competition and to winning. 'Deliberate play' becomes 'deliberate practice' as young players focus increasingly on improving their levels of performance and increase the frequency and intensity of their training.

If the player is ready to focus on one sport, and to serious and intense training and competition, they move to the 'investment phase'. At this point, the predominant motivation for continuing to play is to win. If they do not wish to continue to this stage, they need not leave sport, as there are opportunities for them to carry on playing recreationally.

Côté and Hay's model has a somewhat different focus to Balyi's; while the latter has a clear concern with the development of elite performers, the former considers more general socialisation into sport. That said, both models are clearly developmental, and allow for different types of sports performance, including elite and recreational levels. Both also seem to presuppose some sort of collaborative and mutually supportive roles for schools and sports groups. Côté and Hay's approach has the virtue of acknowledging that not all players, including talented players, necessarily wish to progress to elite performance, but ought not to be lost from the system. In this regard, their model reflects most closely the recent developments currently taking place within the UK (discussed at the start of this chapter). They also offer an interesting reference point for the inclusive, developmental and school-based approach being advocated in this book.

Thinking about talent development in PE

Talent development in PE has an interesting role within initiatives like EiC and PESSCL. To some extent, PE can be seen as a bridge between the worlds of education and sport. The precise nature of the relative relationships – physical education/sport and physical education/education – is a contested and highly contentious one (Murdoch, 1990), and nowhere is this more apparent than in discussions concerning development of high ability in these areas. An apparent inability to articulate these relationships and draw consensus seems to have resulted in a great deal of uncertainty regarding the aims, methods and foci of talent development in physical education (Bailey *et al.*, 2004). Guidance is readily available on identifying and developing talented pupils within an educational domain – such as the importance of recognising potential ability, as well as current performance (Freeman, 1998), the value of seeking out and supporting underachieving students (Montgomery, 2000) and the need to provide enriching activities both after school and during the school day, as part of good, differentiated practice (Eyre and Lowe, 2002). However, this has been in danger of being overshadowed by apparently contradictory practices associated with elite sport (Abbott *et al.*, 2002; Bailey *et al.*, 2004). Indeed, conventional thought seems to have settled on the assumption that talent development in physical education and sport are synonymous in that similar processes in the main dominated by sport are used in both areas (Beashel, 2002; Fisher, 1996).

In the chapters that follow, we suggest a different way of thinking about talent development in PE.

Summary

- Schools must provide suitable challenge and appropriate support for their most able pupils.
- Appropriate provision can enhance motivation and improve behaviour.
- There are many agencies that can help teachers with this work.
- LEAs, as well as schools, have a duty to support the education of more able pupils.
- Ofsted teams expect to see suitable provision for the most able. It is an inclusion issue.
- School policy, with regard to more able children, must be reflected in practice.

CHAPTER 2

Departmental policy and approach

Equity and excellence – an inclusive approach

PE holds a unique position within the world of gifted and talented education, a position that can be characterised by the twin principles of excellence and equity. On the one hand PE must enable practitioners to identify and provide for the needs of individual children, whilst on the other, it is seen as a necessary foundation for future elite performance and international success. Like all school-based gifted and talented education however, PE should celebrate the development of every pupil's achievement.

Whilst most teachers and writers on the subject distinguish between physical education and sport, central guidance to schools usually does not. Ambiguity surrounding the dual role of PE has provoked a variety of understandings as to what teachers are expected to do with their talented pupils. Our own research suggests that many view this dual role as a source of some concern, not least with regard to the modes of provision normally associated with the different goals. This table usefully simplifies some of the differences.

	Physical education	Sport
When?	Curriculum time	Extracurricular and out-of-school
Who leads?	PE teachers	Some contribution from PE teachers, but increased role for external sports coaches
Who benefits?	All suitable pupils	Only those able to access opportunities
Why?	Meeting pupils' educational needs	Meeting organisations' representative needs

Distinctions need to be made within the talent development process to enable satisfactory outcomes for children excelling in both PE and sport. A sole reliance on a sport-based approach could cause significant problems, such as:

- out-of-school programmes are less able to provide for all pupils, irrespective of gender, ethnicity or socioeconomic background

- sports-based programmes, with their focus on performance, can overlook other abilities, reflected in the National Curriculum for Physical Education (NCPE), such as leadership, knowledge and understanding

- performance-based programmes ignore pupils who are potentially talented but who, due to lack of opportunity or support, are currently underachieving.

Recent reports (Ofsted, 2004; DfES, 2001) suggest that gifted and talented provision should also combine in-school learning with complementary opportunities out of school hours. However, although the potential for overlap within such a system is apparent, the need to differentiate between the two is crucial, to provide for children in an equitable way and also to ensure excellence is nurtured effectively. As talent development systems in sport are well developed, albeit at times fairly complicated in nature, the focus for the following sections will be primarily based on physical education in an attempt to redress the imbalance.

A multi-dimensional approach to developing talent in PE

To gain an understanding of the different abilities that pupils may possess and exhibit within the subject area, it is perhaps more convenient to view these abilities as components of PE. Rather than answering questions such as 'what is PE?', looking more closely at 'what is done in PE?' and in a typical PE lesson at 'what types of talent or abilities are seen?' will provide a clearer picture of what students can or have the potential to do.

The last question can be answered by mapping out different abilities seen in a typical PE lesson.

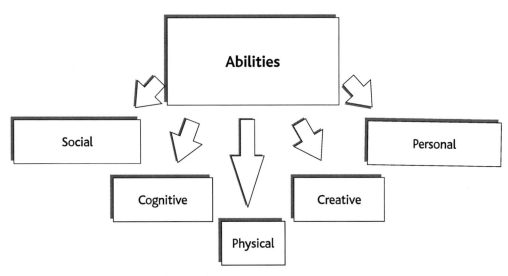

A multi-abilities approach to developing talent

Although physical ability is recognised by identifying high levels of performance, other abilities that are embedded within the NCPE four core strands (acquiring and developing skills, selecting and applying skills, tactics and compositional ideas etc.) and valued aspects of PE per se are identified as well.

In practice, should the defining abilities as proposed be accepted as the foundation for talent development, pupils could be identified as demonstrating, or having the potential to demonstrate, high levels of competency in a wide range of ability domains leading to a number of possible outcomes.

Ability	Definition	Possible outcomes
Physical	Often understood as skill or fitness related ability, this describes the pupil who has specific physical ability associated with high level physical performance. A pupil with high levels of physical ability may exhibit excellence in stamina, speed, reaction, flexibility, coordination, etc.	• High levels of fundamental movement ability • Elite performers • Physical ability across all six activity areas • High marks within practical components of examination PE
Creative	A 'style' of intelligence with a pupil displaying alternative responses to set stimuli, a broad analysis vocabulary and innovative tactics and skills.	• Innovative game tacticians • Problem solvers • Choreographers
Cognitive	The pupil's ability to transfer skills, concepts and applications between and within activities demonstrating a superior awareness of the influence of space in terms of positioning and dominance. A high level of understanding of key principles of sports and an ability to present this effectively.	• Teachers • Coaches • High marks within theoretical components of examination PE
Personal	Pupils with a high level of intra-personal ability are well-motivated and have a constructive approach to achieving their goals. They will also regulate their own learning, set themselves goals and practise hard in their own context (coaching, leading or playing). A well-motivated pupil of average ability may be more successful than a de-motivated pupil of higher ability.	• Elite performers • Teachers • Coaches • Success within examination PE • High level of reward
Social	The pupil's ability to interact with others, demonstrating excellent communication skills and strong leadership qualities within a range of environments. An interpersonal deficiency may also exist in some pupils whereby they are unable to fulfil their potential as a result of the deficiency, for example, by not being able to relate to team members.	• Elite performers (particularly in team environments) • Coaches • Teachers • Expedition leaders

Of course, the question could be asked that to identify talent in physical education should we not be using the National Curriculum and, more specifically, the four core strands as the identifiable features of a talented pupil in physical education? The five named abilities are designed to complement the National Curriculum in that they use key features of the four core strands and make them more explicit to enable teachers to recognise talent more effectively, and subsequently provide for those pupils in a more refined, detailed and systematic way. An example of how the National Curriculum core strands work alongside the abilities framework can be seen in the following table.

National Curriculum strands	Physical education abilities	Examples
1. Acquiring and developing skills	• Physical ability is revealed through a pupil's competence and fitness to perform a range of physical activities.	• The pupil demonstrates excellent levels of skill and technique which are built on a foundation of health and activity related fitness.
2. Selecting and applying skills, tactics and compositional ideas	• Social ability is exhibited in social contexts, and is the basis of leadership, teamwork and similar concepts.	• Sophisticated interpersonal skills allow the pupil to evaluate and improve others' performance as well as motivate and encourage their peers.
	• Personal ability underpins an individual's capacity for self-regulation, self-belief and commitment to mastery.	• The pupil is highly motivated, makes decisions readily, and is able to learn from success and failure in a self-regulated manner.
3. Evaluating and improving performance	• Cognitive ability is shown in planning and compositional settings, as well as knowledge and understanding of central physical educational concepts.	• The pupil is able to exert significant influence within a game due to their high levels of tactical knowledge and understanding.
4. Knowledge and understanding of fitness and health	• Creative ability is evidenced when a learner responds to challenges and tasks with fluency, originality and sensitivity to problems.	• The pupil responds in new ways to a range of stimuli which ultimately increases the chances of success within the activity.

Role of the G&T PE coordinator

Although talent development is simplistic in its aim the policies and processes linked to this aim require thought and imagination. It has already been outlined that a number of principles, not always in harmony with each other, form the backbone of talent development in PE. The person responsible for the design of a policy for talent development in PE, and its subsequent implementation, needs to be aware of a range of themes, principles and strategies that will help them to provide a rich, equitable and progressive talent development programme.

So as to be able to recognise the scope of the task involved in adopting the position of person with responsibility for talent development in PE, the job description opposite has been developed.

Principles of departmental policy

Previous sections of this chapter show the establishment of key features of the talent development process. It is important now that the ethos and underlying principles of this approach are assimilated into a series of working practices that can be shared and owned by the whole department. These practices could otherwise be known as the 'principles of policy' and for the purpose of this section the term 'policy' is defined as the systematic and dynamic application of theory into practice. Although over-prescription should be clearly avoided, to allow for the school's own individualities and maintain the professionalism of teachers who have a highly informed perception of the children they teach, a common set of principles can be formulated as a foundation for talent development policy in a physical education department. The four key areas of policy development to which key principles can be applied are:

1. an educational approach to talent development in PE

2. identification and selection

3. teaching and provision

4. professional development.

In each section reference is made to departmental responsibilities and also how pupils can be actively engaged in the talent development process.

1. An educational approach to talent development in PE

The department:

- ensures that talent development policy for physical education is embedded within physical education and whole-school G&T policies

- is fully aware of the distinctive nature of physical education, and ensures that talent development in physical education maintains its educational focus

Job description for a G&T PE coordinator

Description of responsibility	Examples
Design, implement and monitor a departmental policy relating to developing talent in PE	Refer to later section on policy for more details
Ensure that all departmental staff are fully involved in the identification of, and provision for, talented pupils in PE	Departmental meetings/school INSET is used to monitor and standardize the identification and provision processes
Develop links with external talent development support agencies effectively, including the effective use of non-specialist teachers, qualified coaches and adults other than teachers (AOTTs)	A needs-based professional development programme is implemented to enable external support agencies to function effectively
Be responsible for supporting the professional development requirements of all members of the department and ensure success criteria for talent development programmes are directly related to professional development opportunities	Advertise courses within the department specific to their needs. Audit pupil opportunities at key times to assess the impact of staff attendance/development in relation to pupils accessing, and succeeding at, activities
Liaise with the school G&T coordinator, and be responsible for cascading any talent development related information to other members of the department	Have regular input into departmental meetings and act as a mediator between school G&T coordinator and the PE department
Be responsible for a support programme for talented pupils in PE	Individual education plans are discussed and formulated for each identified talented pupil and mentors are designated accordingly
Ensure that talent identification processes are (1) transparent and (2) equitable and all pupils are aware of the process of talent identification	(1) Identification criteria is clearly displayed for all pupils to access and parents are also informed within the school prospectus (2) Pupils with special educational needs, disabilities or medical conditions are interviewed in order to assess accessibility issues
Be responsible for establishing, monitoring and reviewing a database for talented pupils in PE	Information from the database is used to inform identification and provision practices and contribute to the reporting procedures within school
Liaise with feeder schools to facilitate a seamless transition between KS2 and KS3 for talented children in PE	Information received from primary schools is used as a platform for subsequent identification and provision strategies
Establish a range of forums for talent development strategies to be aired and discussed	Parents of talented pupils in PE are invited to school to discuss ways in which they can support their children effectively
Assess the impact of talent development strategies on mainstream curricular provision	Observe colleagues, and be observed when delivering specific strategies for talented pupils in PE to assess the effectiveness of the provision
Ensure a varied identification process is adopted	Integrate self and peer assessment into identification processes
Act as liaison with other subject areas within the school and other schools' PE departments in sharing best practice and clustering activities in talent development	Talented pupils in PE are able to access programmes of activities in which they work alongside other pupils with gifts and talents from other subject areas and schools
Ensure pathways for extending their talent to out-of-school environments are established and clearly outlined to pupils	External speakers are invited into assemblies to advertise their services and a notice board is used to display local events and opportunities

- collaborates productively with a range of key partners in the design and implementation of talent development programmes.

Pupils:

- recognise that physical education talent development policy and practices are part of a whole-school G&T programme
- are fully aware of, and involved in, physical education talent development policies within their school, and understand how these policies impact on their physical education and general school experiences.

2. Identification and selection

The department:

- is explicit about the expectations of pupils aspiring to be identified as talented in physical education
- devises/formulates strategies to identify diverse abilities, in order to provide pupils with opportunities to reveal strengths in a variety of domains
- organises opportunities for sharing experiences and moderating the talent identification process
- monitors talent cohort composition to ensure equitable identification practices are taking place including disabled pupils, pupils' socioeconomic status, special educational needs or medical conditions.

Pupils:

- are fully aware of the strategies employed to identify talent in physical education
- are identified for their abilities across a wide range of physical education contexts
- assess and nominate themselves and their peers in a range of environments to contribute to the talent identification process.

3. Teaching and support

The school ensures that:

- curricular provision is adapted, modified or replaced to meet the distinctive needs of talented pupils in PE
- a portfolio of evidence is gathered during identification to inform and direct the provision process

- the focus of provision in schools for talented pupils in PE is firmly located within curricular PE, and reflects NC requirements.

Pupils:

- are fully aware of their strengths and areas for development, and the contribution provision strategies can make to this development

- engage in a structured programme of activities in which they work alongside pupils with gifts and talents in PE and other subject areas

- are offered opportunities to discuss the impact of their talents on their personal lives with mentors and the PE G&T coordinator.

4. Professional development

The school:

- uses increased opportunities for pupils as success criteria for the evaluation of the impact of professional development activities

- collaborates with other schools and national bodies to remain informed of current initiatives related to talent development in PE

- organises a range of ongoing subject-specific professional development

- ensures that PE staff are all involved in the identification of and provision for talented pupils in PE

- provides a comprehensive and needs-based professional development programme for all teachers and adults-other-than-teachers (AOTT) involved in the development of talented pupils in PE.

Cycle of policy implementation

Whereas some educational policies assume a fairly standard starting point for the implementation of a particular directive; here, due to the varying impact of EiC and school sport partnerships across schools, a variety of potential departmental starting points must be recognised.

However, formulating policy at the outset will help a PE department gain a real sense of ownership over the process of talent development, from the initial design right through to its provision and refinement. The diagram overleaf represents the cyclic approach to talent development and reiterates the themes of each part of the process.

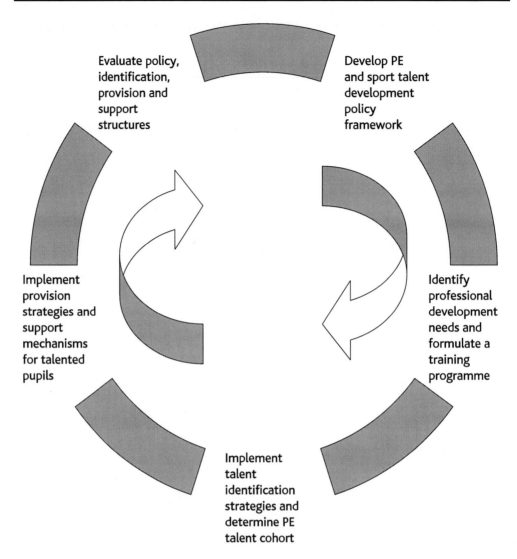

The cycle of talent development in physical education

A policy outline for talent development in physical education – maybe different, but not more!

It is the intention of this section to present workable and manageable guidance for the development of policy that seeks to redefine some areas of curriculum practice to provide more opportunities for talented pupils.

It is certainly not the intention for practitioners within PE to view the design and subsequent application of such policy as something additional to their current provision. In many instances, schools will already have a fairly sophisticated talent development programme that may simply need packaging in a more effective way to guide teachers and pupils more efficiently. Whilst the sections above have discussed in detail the themes and underlying principles related to the development of a talent development policy in PE, there remains a need for a further tier of application to be outlined to offer departments a clear working framework for policy design. Therefore, the following paragraphs will apply the principles and themes presented previously into a policy outline that will allow departments to engage in a well informed and progressive talent development programme.

Gifted and talented whole-school policies have been offered before by various authors (Eyre, 2001; Hymer and Michel, 2002; George, 2003) and for the sake of compatibility with existing school systems some of the central themes of these policies will be cascaded into the development of a physical education departmental policy outline.

Rationale

- Why are we developing talent in PE? (For example, to raise standards of achievement within PE, to create sporting pathways, as part of pre-inspection self-evaluation?)

- Who will benefit, and in what ways – what outcomes are we aiming for?

- How does the PE talent development rationale fit into whole-school-policy G&T statements?

- Is the current form of talent development meeting, or not meeting, expectations?

Aims

As a department what are we looking to achieve through the talent development programme – what will the students get out of it?

- a challenging, stimulating and innovative environment

- individually tailored talent development programme enhanced through sophisticated identification, provision and support processes

- the holistic development of students using a multi-dimensional approach

- the opportunity to succeed, and experience reward, for exhibiting a range of abilities

- lifelong participation in physical activity at their chosen level of involvement

- preparation for stepping onto pathways for development in specific sports

- accreditation and recognition for their efforts (e.g. JSLA, CSLA, GCSE, AS, A level PE).

Definition

Who do we define as talented in PE and sport? How can we make the definition we use as simple yet appropriate for the inclusion of a wide range of students with high ability in PE?

Here, for the purpose of clarity, and to ensure principles of equity and excellence are being applied, there are two distinct pathways – one for those students with high ability in curricular **physical education** and one for those with high ability in one or more **sports**.

- Talented students in physical education demonstrate ability over and above that of their peers in the first instance through a high National Curriculum level and then within one or more specific abilities (i.e. cognitive, social, physical, creative and personal).

- Talented students in physical education may demonstrate high levels of ability in one or more activity areas.

- Talented students in sport demonstrate ability over and above that of their peers within the representative honours framework (i.e. national governing bodies, school, city/town/county/region/area/national/international).

- Some potentially talented students may be underachieving or failing to reach their potential as a result of certain issues that prevent their talent from being manifested. (For example, pressure of competition, lack of parental support, lack of finances. The following chapter, on recognising potential, offers more guidance on this area.)

- Talented students may bring exceptional skills from other areas of the curriculum that enhance their ability to succeed in physical education.

Identification

Once definitions of talent or potential have been agreed how do we allow the specified talent to be revealed?

Systems

- Auditing systems are employed to recognise and monitor out-of-school talent (for example, school sport survey).

- Opportunities exist for self, peer and parental nomination.

- Existing methods of assessment are used to enhance planned refinements to talent identification systems.

- Student tracking profiles are established through means of a database that allow student progress to be assessed and monitored.

- Standardisation of the identification process is conducted at regular intervals during the identification phase.

- Curricular provision, including balance of content, duration of units of work and delivery style, is audited and monitored to assess the effectiveness of meeting talented students' needs.

Strategies

Detailed information on specific identification strategies is provided in subsequent sections within this chapter. The effective use of identification strategies may be best viewed within a short-, medium- and long-term developmental planning framework which should also address the manageability of the programme. The following questions provide a structure for the effective adoption of one, or more, identification strategies.

- **What strategy(ies)?**
  With specific reference to your agreed definitions, and principles involved in the process of identification, which strategy meets the needs of the students?

- **Why?**
  Does this fulfil the immediate needs of talented students? Does this particular strategy allow you to gauge the accuracy of your definition and engage all members of the department in the agreed approach?

- **With whom?**
  Year group, Key Stage, boys, girls, GCSE students, specific sports players (county, national performers)

- **When and where?**
  The most appropriate term, activity area, time of the day, frequency of delivery, facility, location.

- **Are there any staffing issues?**
  Who will deliver the strategy? Opportunities for team teaching, shadowing, clustered activities, sharing resources, cascading of information. Issues related to expertise, confidence, experience, levels of challenge.

- **Are there any resourcing issues?**
  Are there financial implications for adopting a specific strategy – staff development, equipment, resource development?

- **Are there any whole-school issues?**
  How do(es) the chosen strategy (ies) align with whole-school G&T practices? Are there opportunities for cross-curricular identification information to be shared? Is the whole-school G&T co-ordinator in agreement with the proposed plan of action?

- **What next?**
  Design an action plan in alignment with existing departmental planning frameworks which allows the effective implementation of the identification strategy to become part of the whole departmental planning process.
  Be realistic: use short-, medium- and long-term ideals and adopt identification strategies that suit the definitions that have been developed.

Teaching and support

Systems

- Provision strategies relate directly to the abilities that have been identified.

- Standardisation opportunities are organised frequently during the provision phase.

- Assessment of current provision is conducted to identify opportunities for compatibility with proposed provision approach.

- Evaluation of provision strategies is used to inform future provision.

- Students are provided with opportunities for self-regulation through exercises such as mind mapping, action planning and assessments of time management.

- Students are engaged in discussion to elaborate on the demands placed upon them as a result of being included on the talent development programme.

Organisational responses

- **Acceleration**

    a. Opportunities are given to talented pupils to work with pupils older than themselves. There are logistical problems here considering the constraints of timetabling but the rewards are easily recognisable.

    b. Talented pupils are given work normally given to older pupils. This could be within the National Curriculum and perhaps using the QCA Schemes of Work and/or using GCSE PE with a Year 9 group.

    c. Early examination entry is offered for talented pupils in GCSE/A level PE and/or Dance, Duke of Edinburgh Schemes and awards such as Junior Sport Leaders Award (note: some governing bodies restrict the entry age for some examinations).

    d. Pupils are given opportunities to practise with, and compete alongside and against, older pupils during extracurricular activities. Note: some governing bodies advise that by a certain age it is not recommended that children from differing ages compete against each other, e.g. rugby, whereas athletics as an extracurricular activity will offer a range of opportunities for accelerating the pupil's learning in this environment.

    e. Where an acceleration strategy is adopted the social and emotional impact on the talented pupil is monitored (this will normally be conducted by an appointed mentor).

- **Mentoring**

    a. Mentors are appointed on a case-by-case basis for talented pupils in PE and sport. (For talented pupils in sport the Junior Athlete Education programme (JAE) is well established within the school sport partnership network, and this provides support for athletes who have represented their county or above in one or more sports. For more information on the JAE programme, visit www.youthsporttrust.org.

b. Mentoring groups will be based on different ratios, ranging from one-to-one, to larger groups of talented pupils with a single mentor, depending on the needs of the pupil involved.

c. Mentors will be drawn from a variety of sources including teachers from other subject areas, those adults responsible for the pastoral welfare of pupils (e.g. heads of year, assistant head teachers, behaviour improvement teamworkers, learning mentors already within school), people from local businesses and local coaches and others involved in sport.

d. For talented pupils in sport, the most significant focus for discussion with mentors is likely to be the maintenance of the work/sport/life balance.

e. For talented pupils in PE, mentors are used to direct and enhance their specific ability (e.g. for those pupils identified as having high levels of cognitive ability in PE, mentors could provide support for how their talents could be used in other curricular areas).

● **Grouping**

a. Grouping of pupils is conducted on a year-by-year and, where necessary, teaching group-by-teaching group basis.

b. Large scale grouping of pupils (i.e. whole/half year groups) will be used (setting, streaming) where appropriate if it is recognised that talented pupils will be challenged more effectively by using this particular system.

c. Small scale grouping of pupils within a teaching group will be used to match the needs of pupils with specific abilities that are determined by success within an activity area, e.g. athletic activities, or by type of ability, e.g. creative, physical, cognitive groups.

Pedagogic responses

● **Short- and medium-term planning** specifically targets provision for talented pupils.

● **Differentiation** is used as the central focus of provision for talented pupils with specific reference to the different:

a. style of presentation to match pupils' varying learning and thinking styles

b. use of resources, such as technological equipment (e.g. PCs, laptops, whiteboards, cameras, recording equipment, CDs) and various forms of stimulus (e.g. task cards, photographs) although more does not always necessarily equate to better here, as limiting equipment and forms of stimulus may challenge talented pupils more effectively in the creative way they may use it

c. teaching style, particularly when addressing the needs of pupils across the ability spectrum (e.g. if a command or didactic style of teaching were employed, this would not be productive in terms of providing for a pupil with high levels of creativity)

d. use of questioning (more open than closed) and probing to gauge the pupil's understanding of the topic

e. levels of challenge within homework tasks set.

● **Self-regulation** is advocated through the use of a learning portfolio maintained by the pupil and monitored by the teacher.

Extracurricular activities

In-school and out-of-school extracurricular activities provide opportunities for pupils to enhance and build on learning which has occurred during school.

● **During in-school extracurricular activities:**

a. Curricular planning and delivery suggest pathways for talented pupils in PE to enrich their ability through extracurricular activities.

b. Information is provided for all pupils through a dedicated display board that documents a range of extracurricular activities both in school and beyond into the community.

c. Opportunities are offered for pupils with a range of abilities to extend their experiences within curricular PE (e.g. pupils with high levels of social ability may be employed as coaches during practices and/or fixtures, and they may also be offered the opportunity of accessing a Junior Sports Leaders Award).

d. There is enough flexibility to modify extracurricular activities to suit the needs of the current cohort of pupils.

e. Within the planning process, factors affecting participation in extracurricular activities are considered, particularly in relation to the pupil's age, gender, socioeconomic status and ethnicity.

f. On issues of fairness and transparency, other factors are also considered such as the timing of the activity (after-school activities may preclude some pupils who travel home using school transport), the nature of the activity in terms of open access and whether there is a balance of activities in terms of their orientation towards teams or individuals.

g. Selection of talented individuals for specific school sports teams takes into account the relative age effect of children and offers opportunities for pupils to compete who have birth dates spanning across the year.

h. Talented pupils are encouraged to represent the views of their peers by applying for a position on the school council.

i. Talented pupils are engaged in a wide range of activities related to the PE and sporting life of the school such as the production of a PE and sports newsletter which pupils could design, edit, contribute articles towards and publish.

j. Pupils showing potential in specific activities or within certain ability domains are encouraged to attend extracurricular activities and their progress is monitored and recorded by their subject teacher.

k. Workshops that address the widespread needs of talented pupils in PE are held and these workshops cover such areas as nutrition, preparation for competition; and for parents, advice on how best to support their talented child.

- **During out-of-school extracurricular activities:**

a. Sports trips, residential visits and visits to higher education institutions are organised to enhance the experiences of talented pupils.

b. In liaison with a number of other local schools, cluster activities are organised at a central location so that talented pupils in PE have the opportunity of working alongside talented pupils from other schools.

c. Coaches involved in specific sports from organisations outside of school are invited into school to present information on local, regional and national opportunities for participation (this can be achieved on an individual basis or through the hosting of an open event organised at school for interested parties to display their services collectively).

d. Communication between the PE department and sports organisations is instigated and frequently maintained by the PE G&T coordinator.

e. Pupils are regularly audited to assess their level of involvement in out-of-school extracurricular activities and this information is used to enhance and complement the in-school extracurricular activities programme.

Continuing professional development

As the cyclic model of talent development shown earlier in this chapter demonstrates, continuing professional development is recognised as an integral feature of the talent development process. CPD needs for teachers related to talent development exist within a number of distinct fields as expressed in the diagram overleaf.

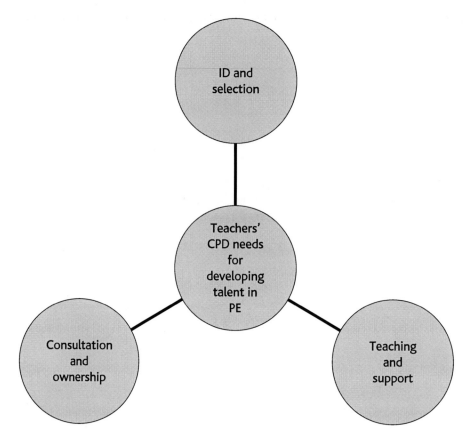

Teachers' CPD needs for developing talent in PE

Identification and selection

It has been recognised that identification is the most complex and problematic area of gifted and talented development (Freeman, 1998; DfEE, 1999a; Ofsted, 2004). For this reason once the issues surrounding the policy development aspects of identification have been grappled with and formulated the next step is to ensure a rigorous process of professional development to ensure equitable practice throughout the process. CPD at this stage needs to be reflexive to the needs of practitioners as they journey through the process of identification and selection. Every school and teacher will have their own individual needs commensurate with the demands of their talented pupils, however, the following list should provide generic areas for CPD content related to the identification and selection of talented pupils in PE:

- teaching strategies for talented pupils

- defining talent in PE and sport – what are the differences?

- characteristics of talented pupils in PE

- informing talented pupils and their parents about their talent

- the sensitive handling of entry onto, and exit from, the talented cohort

- school requirements for identification – compatibility with other subject areas G&T identification and whole-school policy guidelines

- maintaining the database of talented pupils.

Teaching and support

To respond to the unique needs of talented pupils, teachers need to be given opportunities to explore methods of stimulating learning in different ways within lessons. The identification and provision strategies outlined within Chapters 3 and 4 act as starting points and can be used by teachers as frameworks for development but there needs to be a further consideration of the types of teaching environments talented pupils will thrive in. The accumulation of these teaching skills will not happen by chance and therefore requires specific intervention. Intervention at a teaching level could consist of:

- opportunities to 'team teach' talented pupils and discuss outcomes and future intentions

- shadowing teachers who are more experienced in providing for talented pupils in PE

- exploring ways in which existing planning can be modified to cater for talented pupils more effectively

- standardising evidence of talent with colleagues (video, records of assessment)

- the use of action research to explore teacher and pupil effectiveness

- opportunities to lead the development of less experienced staff in talent provision

- access to working groups established to evaluate provision practices

- exploring pathway development opportunities for talented pupils in PE to step into sport.

Consultation and ownership

With the plethora of recent initiatives in PE it is imperative that the design and implementation of talent development policy and practices is managed in a way that accounts for the increasing pressure on teachers and subject departments. In practice, this will mean that consensus of agreement is reached at every stage of the talent development process and lead-in times associated with progressing around the cycle of implementation are realistic and reasonable. This ethos reflects earlier sections on not particularly 'more' but maybe 'different' and this approach should facilitate a positive outlook towards talent development so that practitioners do not feel as if they are having to contend with yet another initiative. In this respect CPD programmes for talent development should explore opportunities for merging with existing CPD by emphasising certain strategic elements of the planned content to make them more appropriate to a talent development environment. For example, overlapping principles can be found in generic CPD content related to assessment, extracurricular activities, curriculum design, resource purchasing, grouping and inclusion.

CHAPTER 3

Recognising talent and potential

Underlying principles of talent identification in PE

Fundamentally, the process of identification relies heavily on a *stimulating*, *challenging* and *revealing* environment whereby the various abilities of all children can be readily manifest.

Employing the notion of allowing pupils the opportunities to reveal their abilities affords pupils with a range of abilities the chance to shine. In doing so curricular provision can be effectively targeted and the needs of those pupils identified across the range of abilities can be more easily met.

The previous chapters have outlined an understanding of the definitions of talent in PE in preparation for the ensuing identification process. However, to be effective such an identification process must be transparent, fair, rigorous and continuous.

Transparency

To be effective, all communication routes between involved individuals and organisations must be transparent. Firstly, if pupils are to assess their own development and aspirations, identification policies and practices need to be clearly documented and displayed. Informing parents and perhaps coaches of the nature of the child's development will enable them to make their own contribution to the well-being of the talented pupil. Parents and coaches are essential parts of a talented pupil's system of support, in that they can actively assist in the monitoring, evaluation and support of the child, addressing in particular the notion of school–life balance.

Fairness

Although there may always be exceptions, a standardised and agreed form of identification must be applied consistently throughout the process. To counteract the potential for discriminatory practices, barriers to access and opportunity must be considered alongside a rationale for the identification process. Where pupils may exit the talent development programme the reasons for them doing so, along with possibilities for re-engagement, must be clearly outlined for the pupil.

Rigour

Although research does not support the claim that talented pupils are socially or emotionally different to any other child, they do have very specific educational needs and may experience issues related to their identification as being talented. Therefore, a clearly articulated individualised support programme needs to parallel the identification procedure.

Continuity

The cycle of identification, selection, provision and support is never complete and the composition of the talented cohort should reflect this. Lessons learned from adopting certain principles and practices should be constantly fed back into the process to inform future direction and development.

Recognising potential

Identification and recognition of potential is no simple task in PE. It can easily be forgotten when more obvious current achievements are so readily observable. Indeed, Ofsted has cited the identification of pupils with potential as an area requiring development. (Ofsted, 2004; DfES, 2001)

Within a PE environment, current achievement is also measurable by locally and nationally referenced norms (i.e. Amateur Athletic Association guidelines for representing county, regional and national associations). Whilst PE has the occasional luxury of relying on guidelines produced by external agencies and the benefit of a level-based national curriculum, the subject area does not have the same information to monitor potential as some other subjects. Whilst other subject areas can rely on Cognitive Abilities Tests (CATS), National Tests (SATS), Middle Years Information System (MIDYiS), Year 11 Information System (YELLIS) and the Autumn Package to monitor underachievement, the realisation of potential such data provides is of limited use within a practical field such as PE.

The problem with identifying potential concerns how we actually see it. Whilst sporadic moments, expressions of talent that might point to potential are easily noticed; in reality, we are not interested in seeing potential but rather recognising what is preventing the pupil from fulfiling their potential. Therefore, it might be easier when considering how to best harness potential to consider the following formula:

Productivity (performance) = Potential – interference (barriers)

(Adapted from Steiner, 1972)

This formula suggests that pupils' potential to succeed (or be productive) is always influenced by the interference they encounter which prevents them from fulfiling that potential (or maximising their productivity).

In PE, *interference* can take many forms which *impact* on a pupil's ability to fulfil their potential.

Interference and impact

Interference	Impact
Lack of parental support – ● informational ● tangible ● emotional	● Pupil does not have the opportunity to deepen knowledge and understanding in their home environment. ● Pupil does not participate in lessons due to not having PE clothing and equipment. ● Pupil does not receive recognition for success and fails to understand the reason for winning/succeeding.
Not being able to access facilities, equipment, etc.	● Pupil finds it difficult to practise and develop newly acquired skills in a stimulating and realistic environment and fails to have their passion for an activity nurtured.
Incompatible teaching style	● Certain abilities will not be harnessed if teaching is primarily conducted in a particular way. For example, if a child has high levels of creativity but their PE lessons are taught in a predominantly didactic manner they are not going to be able to fulfil their creative potential.
Limited curriculum design	● If the curriculum is biased towards a particular activity area then pupils with potential in other areas are at a disadvantage which may lead to certain pupils becoming disillusioned with their preferred choice of activity.
Personal deficiencies (poor levels of self-esteem, self-belief and self-regulation)	● The pupil is not motivated to participate fully in activities, which could lead to their isolation and a reduction in their enjoyment of the activity leading to non-participation.
Social deficiencies (e.g. inability to relate to others)	● A pupil who finds it difficult to relate to their peers, particularly in a team situation, is not going to fulfil their potential as they will not function effectively as a part of the team.

Developing talent in PE is not always a 'bed of roses', and it is the acknowledgement of the existence of many forms of interference that will ultimately allow for a more informed process of intervention at the identification stage. Indeed, it may be expedient to attempt to assess a pupil's potential in relation to interference they may be experiencing, in advance of the identification stage. Further details of strategies that can be used to understand levels of potential more effectively will be outlined later in this chapter.

Frameworks for identifying talented pupils in PE

Each method of identifying the very able distinguishes a somewhat different group of children, with possibly different consequences for their self-concepts and education.

(Freeman, 1998: 4)

Currently, schools in the UK are adopting a systematic model of 'defining, identifying and providing' (DIP) that seeks to clearly identify gifted (excelling in academic subjects) and talented (excelling in physical education, sport and the creative arts) pupils for further support and specialised provision. Tilsley (1995) has offered an alternative and potentially more inclusive model whereby provision is offered, evaluated and subsequently modified to address students' needs. This model of 'providing-evaluating-providing' (PEP) reflects more closely a multidimensional approach to talent development, as it affords opportunities for a range of abilities to emerge.

It is likely, however, that any department embarking on a talent development scheme will undoubtedly utilise both models. In effect this would mean that before the process of defining, and subsequently identifying, talent has occurred using the DIP model a certain amount of provision and evaluation has probably already taken place as part and parcel of everyday best practice within assessment and teaching in PE. This formative, ongoing process of identification is crucial in maximising access and opportunities for pupils who manifest their potential at varying stages of their education and development.

Categories of identification strategies

If the notion that talented children in physical education may possess high levels of ability in one or more areas is to be accepted as previously suggested, then it is important that identification strategies used match this aspiration.

Identification strategies in PE can be grouped into three broad categories, as shown in the table below.

Categories of identification strategies

Category	Explanation	Examples
Relatively generic strategies	assess overall performance or a cluster of core abilities at the same time	differentiation, formative assessment
Activity-specific measures	assessments of performance in different activities	agility, balance, coordination tests in athletic activities, game activities, dance, etc.
Ability-specific strategies	focus on the assessment of the abilities underlying participation and performance in physical education contexts (physical, social, personal, cognitive and creative)	creativity tests, problem solving tasks for social ability

Using multiple identification criteria ensures a diverse talent cohort, which is in keeping with guidelines from central government agencies (e.g. DfES, 2003), and reflects the nature of the subject area more accurately than the purely performance-based identification procedure conventionally found in sport.

Moreover, many of the simplest yet more suitable identification strategies lie at the heart of good generic teaching practice, such as formative assessment and differentiation. However, it may be the case that such generic strategies only provide a broad-brush portrait of a pupil's ability and achievement so, at some stage of the process, there may be a need to focus on specific abilities as part of a more detailed assessment of that pupil's talent.

Using a strategic approach to identify talent in PE

Once abilities inherent within talented pupils in PE (physical, cognitive, social, personal and creative) have been defined, a multidimensional strategic approach facilitating a number of clearly defined pathways for the whole range of abilities can be developed to allow pupils to realise them. Driven by the following principles, it:

- is school-based, and located primarily within curricular PE practice

- is inclusive, both in terms of the range of pupils who will potentially benefit from the provision, and the range of abilities it seeks to identify and develop

- is explicitly linked to the National Curriculum

- reflects current best practice, and seeks to connect this work with established practice in sports development

- goes beyond assessing physical performance to include each of the abilities that underpins talent in PE and sport, such as creativity, interpersonal skills and thinking skills

- offers a portfolio of strategies to teachers, which can be combined and adapted by schools to meet their own priorities.

As there are no absolute scientific methods for identifying talented pupils in PE, the flexibility of a non-prescriptive 'menu' of strategies allows a school to determine the most appropriate course of action for them based on a range of existing factors. These points of consideration include existing:

- talent/very able identification systems

- curriculum provision

- timetabling

- support within lessons

- whole-school and departmental priorities

- facilities

- equipment

- staff expertise

- local support (e.g. clubs).

Identification strategies

Up to this stage this chapter has dealt with the 'why' of the talent identification process – why it is important that we identify in certain ways and perhaps not others.

The following section builds on the concepts and principles outlined so far and provides clear examples of 'how' schools can use a range of strategies to identify talent. These strategies are therefore presented as starting points and representative of a general approach that is both educational and developmental. Each school has its own distinctive needs and challenges, so there is no expectation that every strategy will suit every school. Therefore, readers are encouraged to think about whether each of the individual approaches might be applied, adapted or disregarded in their own context.

Identification strategies are presented by means of an explanation of what the actual strategy is designed to achieve, and this is followed with an example of how the strategy works in a school context by way of a case study or a summary of some of the key issues schools have experienced in implementing the strategy. The vast majority of the strategies have been trialled within schools and evaluations have been conducted to assess their effectiveness.

Many of the strategies have associated resources and teaching materials. These materials have been designed by the school and reflect the approach of the school in response to the needs of the pupils and their environment. Therefore, the example of practice and associated materials is used to demonstrate an example to offer insight rather than absolute universal solutions.

Dynamic assessment

Explanation

Dynamic assessment is a method of assessing progress (Kirschenbaum, 1998). Traditionally, teachers assess learners at the end of period of instruction, but this fails to take account of the different levels of ability among the members of the class before instruction has begun. In other words, end-of-unit assessment gives the teacher an indication of a learner's current performance, but says nothing about their progress and potential to excel. In physical education lessons in particular, all children do not participate on a 'level playing field', as some have considerably greater access to additional coaching, facilities and support than others.

Method

Perhaps the simplest way of administering dynamic assessment is through a 'test-teach-test' (or, more accurately, 'assess-intervene-assess') process. The virtue of approaches like this is that they can offer insight into an individual's 'learnability', the ability to take on and use new skills and understandings, which seems to be a good indicator of potential talent (Kirschenbaum, 1998). It is often more viable to select an activity within an activity area that the pupils are not so familiar with. For example, although some children will bring generic movement skills associated to previously experienced sports, the use of an abstract game (e.g. tchoukball, korfball) will alleviate some of the imbalance of previous experiences. Similarly, creating an unfamiliar teaching environment will facilitate effective dynamic assessment of personal and social ability. Sport education (Siedentop *et al.*, 2004) provides a role-based environment for assessing such abilities and the use of reciprocal teaching will allow children the opportunity to teach others.

Issues

Although dynamic assessment as a method (test-teach-test) can be employed as an identification strategy across any activity area and indeed can concentrate on any ability (e.g. creativity, social etc.), the most productive use of this approach is in environments where previous or ongoing knowledge gained from within related contexts cannot influence the test results. For example, if the process of dynamic assessment was to be applied to the teaching of a unit of work on hockey, previous and ongoing experiences of those involved in playing hockey could affect their initial and post-test results and development through the intervention part of the process.

Example of the strategy in practice

Hungerhill Comprehensive School, Doncaster

Description

The school implements an eight week dynamic assessment scheme of work designed to identify the physical potential of all the pupils in the group. The scheme of work involves a pre-test in week 1 followed by a six week development period and a post-test in week 8. The strategy takes place during curricular time and has been used with groups in Years 9 and 10.

All of the activities focus on fundamental movement skills such as agility, coordination and balance. This allows the teacher to observe the progress of each pupil and gain an understanding of their potential to learn new skills.

Teachers' views

Teachers felt confident in spotting the talented performers at the beginning of the scheme of work:

'Straight away I think you can identify pupils who are talented because they have got those skills. You can see it straight away if you've got a mixed ability class, you can see the ones who can get rhythm, who are light on their feet.'

The dynamic assessment enabled the teachers to also identify the potentially talented pupils in a mixed ability group:

'You can identify the ones who are good, but also pupils who have talent maybe that has not been identified, by doing a little test at the beginning and then doing a test at the end, you can see how greatly they've actually improved by and obviously those who improve quite substantially, we often identify as having talent that they can learn and develop quite quickly.'

The development of fundamental movement skills was greatly valued by the teachers:

'I think it could be applied to all ability groups . . . we've talked about maybe moving it into the Athletics schemes of work because it does work on those specific skills that are required in every sport that you do . . . whether you're a gymnast, an athlete, a games player, everybody does need agility, balance, coordination, speed, you need to be able to react fast in certain situations.'

Pupils' views

Pupils understood the concept of fundamental movement skills and could apply these skills to their own sporting interests:

'It's like coordination mainly which speeds up all your reactions which helps generally in all the sport that I play.'

'In netball, my sport, where you have certain rules against footwork and this kind of helps you co-ordinate it.'

The talented pupils believed that they had improved in the skills throughout the eight-week programme and some pupils felt that they continued to develop after the programme had finished. The introduction of fundamental movement skills into other activity areas has enabled pupils to practise more advanced movements:

'We started off with really simple tasks and once you've been identified they move you on to more complex things.'

Resources

For a sample dynamic assessment short-term plan see Appendix 3.1. Examples of dynamic assessment activities and an associated pupil record card are also provided on the accompanying CD.

Physical assessment

Explanation

Traditional forms of identification through assessment in predominantly performance-based activities can further clarify specific abilities. The use of testing within health-related exercise is a common feature of Physical Education, primarily used to assess fitness and skill-related ability (Cale and Harris, 2005).

Method

A series of assessments could be utilised in the form of skill-related testing, such as agility (Illinois test), reaction (ruler drop test, light board test), balance (stork test) and coordination (juggling, basketball bounce), and fitness testing, such as speed (30m sprint), flexibility (sit and reach test), stamina (Cooper's run, multi-stage fitness test), power (sergeant jump, standing broad jump) and strength (grip dynamometer, flexed arm hang).

The system used for implementing such physical assessments is dependant on a range of factors including:

- number of children to be assessed

- age of children to be assessed

- number of tests to be used

- nature of tests to be used (stamina, strength, speed)

- resources: facilities, specialist equipment (heart rate monitors, timing gates)

- number of staff involved (potential to combine GCSE, BTEC, JSLA students with assessment procedures)

- frequency of opportunities to assess (start of year, termly, end of Key Stage)

- duration.

Issues

Concerns have been expressed about the potential negative effect of what amounts to a 'screening process' and the lack of real use of data gathered for the development of talent when rates of maturation play such a significant role on the child's physical attributes (Cale and Harris, 2002).

Example of the strategy in practice

Lymm High School, Cheshire

Description

The school organised a day of physical testing for all Year 7 pupils at the beginning of their first term. The tests were designed to assess a range of physical fitness components such as strength, power, endurance and flexibility. A cohort of 360 pupils was divided into four groups, of which two groups (divided by sex) were tested simultaneously across different activities. All indoor sports facilities at the school were utilised for the testing and older pupils assisted with the test administration and results. The results provided the school staff individual pupil fitness profiles and whole year group percentile charts.

Teachers' views

It was helpful to have the Year 12 and 13 further education students to help instruct the activities and record the results. The support that students and other staff provided was essential to make the day successful:

'In a school like ours we've got so many pupils coming to us at once and we can't cope in an organised manner if we don't have help . . . it needs staff help, it needs big organisation skills, it needs help from senior management to allow for cover ... having been taken off timetable for five periods.'

There were areas of development in some of the tests used:

'Sit and reach only measures lower back and hamstring flexibility, grip test measures forearm strength, power tests only test leg power.'

However, it was felt that the range of tests selected provided an indication of all-round physical fitness and the schools had the facilities to administer the tests effectively and fairly.

Testing all pupils on the same day maximises the reliability of results:

'In a situation where I've got results all on one day, it's all in the same location, everything is the same (equipment, staff, conditions) there's no outside influences ... it's fair for every pupil.'

Fitness testing helps to identify the talented pupils early:

'We're concerned that we're such a big school of nearly 2000 pupils ... that kids slip through the net for our team sports ... we've got kids coming from a range of primary schools and we've got no idea what they're like ... we can say "you've got great talent across a range of abilities, you should be playing in the rugby, hockey, netball, whatever team, don't go home at 3:10, come and stay in school sport", and we're not going to get pupils only coming to us after 2 or 3 years in school.'

The results not only highlighted the talented pupils but also the pupils with low levels of fitness who may require support from the school and parents. It was felt that this cohort should be offered sporting opportunities and lifestyle education to try and improve their health and fitness.

Pupils' views

Pupils understood the different components of physical fitness and felt that to be talented in PE they had to 'enjoy it' but also be strong and fast with 'good stamina'. They felt the purpose of the day's fitness testing was to learn new skills, learn how to train, to 'see how fit people are' and to allow their teachers to 'put us into groups of ability'. Pupils enjoyed the day off their usual timetable and some felt that the school was trying to help them become better at sport.

Resources

For an activities timetable see Appendix 3.2 and the accompanying CD.

Assessment of creativity

Explanation

Creativity is one of five abilities that can be used to identify talent in PE. It has been suggested that creativity is a 'style' of intelligence (Cropley, 1995), and the application of this intelligence within a PE context could involve pupils completing conventional tasks in a novel way.

Ofsted (2003) sees creative processes as:

- always involving thinking or behaving imaginatively

- using an imaginative activity that is purposeful: that is, it is directed to achieve an objective

- processes that generate something original

- having an outcome that must be of value in relation to the objective.

Methods

Allowing children the opportunities to respond to tasks in novel and innovative ways as well as harnessing their ability to transfer these newly acquired skills across activities is at the heart of developing creativity. Scenario-based testing whereby children are asked to respond to tasks such as 'find as many ways of reaching an end line as possible' with responses involving verbal responses, physical demonstrations and diagrams is just one simple example of how this could be achieved. These responses need to be elicited in a physical, verbal or written manner to meet the child's learning style; by doing this, pupils who have the intelligence to express their creativity but not the physical prowess to demonstrate it have the opportunity to excel.

Issues

Prior to the creativity assessments being used, educational practice may have discouraged a creative approach to learning and conditioned the conventional rather than the radical. The teaching of games is particularly vulnerable to this concept.

The viability and productivity of the demonstration of creativity is contentious – teachers employing creativity assessments will need to make decisions of whether the objective of the activity is being reached.

Resources

For sample short-term plans see the 'Identifying Creativity in Dance' lessons on the accompanying CD.

Differentiation

Explanation

Differentiation, within the context of teaching talented pupils, is at the heart of the most appropriate teaching approach as it facilitates maximum opportunities for 'revealing opportunities'. Bailey (2001) categorises potential differentiation strategies in terms of organisation (grouping; space roles; interaction), presentation (teaching style; response; resources; support), and content (task; pace; level; practice style). Therefore, differentiation enables the pupils to work on tasks and participate in activities appropriate to their ability levels.

Method

In the first instance, the identification of a wide range of abilities is enhanced through the use of a variety of differentiated approaches to teaching. Occasionally a number of differentiated approaches are employed simultaneously to identify talented pupils effectively. The strategy outlined below suggests one example of how this would work in practice.

Issues

As differentiation is so closely related to good teaching practice there may be a tendency to target the improvement of the whole group as the success criteria of the approach. Whilst this improvement obviously remains commendable the development of talented children with a range of high abilities in the group must be viewed as the primary focus of the approach when employed as a talent identification strategy.

Example of the strategy in practice

Priesthorpe Sports College, Leeds

Description

This example features the use of differentiation in a Year 9 girls' rhythmic gymnastics lesson. Here, the teacher provides the pupils with an opportunity to deliver warm-up activities and small group tasks. This allows the teacher to identify those pupils with good cognitive and interpersonal abilities. Following identification by differentiation, the school continues to use a range of differentiation strategies to develop talented pupils in a number of ways (See differentiation as a provision strategy in Chapter 4)

Teachers' views

Allowing the talented girls to teach some of the activities can have a positive effect for all members of the group:

'The higher abilities can practise communication skills more . . . and develop various strands of the curriculum.'

Differentiation by role helps the girls to develop cognitive ability and in particular their knowledge and understanding of movement patterns:

'If you ask them to teach something, they have to break it down (the movement pattern) . . . They are thinking about how they actually do the skill before they teach it to the other groups.'

Pupils' views

The pupils appreciated the opportunity to use a wider range of equipment:

'We get to try out different things to the other groups, so we get to do more.'

'It's more variety, so if we're a bit advanced then we can use all sorts of different equipment and moves and then it looks better because it gives better presentation.'

They felt that it was beneficial for them to work in groups of similar ability:

'And our friends help us because we can watch each other so we can learn more things from each other.'

Experiencing different roles within the group appeared to have a positive effect on the girls' self-esteem

'It also helps you when you're doing like teaching, it makes you feel more responsible and then that helps when you get like older if you need to be leading somebody or something. It helps out in your job plus if you do like a training course sometimes it goes on your record.'

Resources

For a sample short-term plan see 'Differentiation for talented pupils' on the CD.

Qualitative movement analysis

Explanation

This strategy enables both the teacher and the pupil to understand fundamental movement skills ('observable, goal-directed movement patterns', Burton and Miller, 1998, p. 5) to assist in the development of their own and others' performance. The observation of fundamental movement skills in a qualitative manner goes beyond the testing of how fast, how high and how long in that it is concerned with why movement patterns are effective or not and can be used to make suggestions for improvement. Although this particular strategy is targeted at delivery within Key Stage 2 it was deemed as extremely valuable by the participating secondary schools in that the strategy:

- provided a focus for talent development across a number of primary schools and therefore enhanced standardisation of the assessment of talented pupils before their transition to secondary school

- allowed secondary schools the opportunity to develop a stronger working relationship with their primary school counterparts

- impacted upon the quality of talent identification and subsequent provision as the quality of information generated within primary schools had been improved

- considered the longitudinal development of the child over a longer period of time to ensure the Key Stage 2/3 transition was seamless.

Method

How we qualitatively observe movement can be achieved in a number of ways but to remove elements of subjectivity and improve standardisation the use of a resource seems the most appropriate method. In this particular method of qualitative movement analysis the 'Observing Children Moving' CD was used within the framework of a school sports partnership. In the partnership the school sport coordinator uses the resource to allow the teacher to become familiar with the characteristics of early and later motor development patterns associated with various movement skills. This knowledge and understanding can then be used effectively in identifying pupils with good physical ability. Furthermore, allowing pupils to analyse the performance of others may reveal those pupils who have good cognitive ability in understanding the principles of the 'perfect model' and also those with high levels of personal ability in communicating this effectively. The use of younger children to observe, and the fact that the task did not entail the assessment of their peers performing, prevented the personalisation that occasionally occurs when children are asked to comment upon the performance of their peers. This facilitates a positive, objective and very business-like environment where children are more willing to take risks and make mistakes when offering feedback.

Example of the strategy in practice

Oakbank Sports Partnership, Keighley

Introduction: description of study

'Observing Children Moving' (OCM) is a CD package designed to 'promote high-quality movement education and physical education for children aged 3–7 years' (Whitehead and Maude, 2003). This strategy involved trialling OCM as a talent development resource within a specialist sports college partnership and its feeder primary schools. As an evaluative process, the main aim of the research was to obtain feedback from the partnership development manager (PDM), school sport coordinators (SSCos), primary link teachers (PLTs) and primary school teachers regarding their perceptions of the resource and the dissemination process involved.

The project fully acknowledges the original aims and intentions of the OCM software. However, when applied to the context of talent development in PE, the software indicated further potential as an effective resource in the following areas:

1. Talent identification: The teacher uses the resource to improve movement vocabulary (knowledge of movement skills) in order to identify talented pupils more effectively.

2. Talent enrichment: The teacher uses the resource during PE lessons to help explain the 'perfect model' of performance to talented pupils (direct use of resource or use of printed copies of materials).

3. Knowledge and understanding: The teacher allows the pupils to access the resource to develop knowledge and understanding of their own and others' movement skills.

Overall aim

To provide a greater understanding of how OCM could be utilised as a talent development resource in primary school PE.

Methods

The research team at Leeds Metropolitan University worked closely with a sports college partnership in West Yorkshire. Initial contact was made with the PDM at the sports college and a meeting was organised to introduce the project to SSCos. The meeting involved presenting the resource, explaining the aims of the research and outlining the process of delivering (dissemination) and evaluating OCM as a talent development resource in local primary schools.

Dissemination and evaluation process

Dissemination and evaluation of the resource proposed the following five stage process which progressed over a seven-week period.

1. Partnership development manager training: PDM attends talent development training using the OCM CD.

2. School sport coordinator meeting: PDM delivers training to the SSCos within the partnership which involved three activities:
   i. introduction to the dimensions and rationale of the project
   ii. presentation of the OCM resource (using interactive whiteboard/data projector)
   iii. opportunity for SSCos to explore the resource, ask questions and provide initial feedback on the overall project and the resource.

3. Primary school meeting: SSCos liaise with primary schools (primary link teachers where available and primary school class teachers), providing the software and the necessary guidance and support. Progress is monitored by PDM.

4. Implementation: teachers use the resource within the curriculum with the aim to develop talented pupils in physical education. Progress is monitored by PDM.

5. Evaluation meeting: PDM and SSCos meet to evaluate the effectiveness of the resource and dissemination process.

Stage 4 and 5 interview schedules for practitioners were designed according to the following evaluative framework:

1. Background
   - school information
   - year groups/pupils affected

2. Objective of the talent development strategy
   - aims and objectives of using OCM
   - what was the strategy trying to achieve?

3. The talent development strategy
   - what did you do? (method chosen)
   - how did you implement it?
   - which pupils did it affect?
   - further comments about the use of the strategy

4. What impact did the OCM CD have?
   - consider the short-term effects
   - how do you know the strategy made these differences?

5. Evaluation
   - how successful was OCM as a talent development resource?
   - did you achieve your objectives?
   - where do you go from here?
   - were there any unplanned benefits from the implementation of OCM?

Written consent was obtained from all practitioners, pupils and the parents of pupils involved. All participants understood that their involvement was voluntary and that they could withdraw from the research at any time.

SSCos meeting (Stage 2)

The agenda for this meeting consisted of:

1. introduction and briefing of the research aims and project dimensions
2. explanation and demonstration of the resource
3. opportunity for SSCos to explore the resource
4. discussion of methods and potential uses
5. semi-structured interviews with SSCos.

SSCos' perceptions

First impressions

First impressions of OCM was that it was a 'well researched' and 'in-depth resource' which was useful for breaking down movement skills into smaller parts.

'I think it's really good to have a visual resource for both the teachers and the children to look at. Having it explained . . . the different ways in which the resource could be used, I can see it's multi-functional.'

The resource was perceived to be very user friendly and the most attractive features for the group included the 'hotspots' and the 'split-screen' facilities.

Identifying talent

Regarding the identification of talented pupils, some felt that the OCM resource would be particularly useful for newly qualified teachers (NQT) and non-PE specialists to increase their own awareness of motor development. This would enable them to distinguish more effectively between early and late motor patterns and recognise those pupils who were physically talented:

'If there was perhaps an NQT or a teacher that had just started . . . they can use the resource to develop their knowledge and understanding first before they then go in to identifying pupils within their class.'

'It's certainly a valuable resource because observing pupils is very difficult when you've got 30 pupils in a class and to identify the gifted and talented is very difficult without that knowledge and understanding.'

Developing talent

As a provision strategy for talented pupils, perceived strengths of the resource included the visual guidance it could provide for pupils. It was thought that OCM had the potential to enable talented pupils to improve their own performance as a result of viewing and copying the movement examples displayed on the computer screen:

'Some of them will be able to change their performance; perhaps it shows them as very talented to match some of the ones on the CD.'

It was also thought that the visual guidance feature could support opportunities for talented pupils to teach weaker pupils within the class.

Implementation

Regarding the proposed dissemination process, the general opinion was that the information could be cascaded effectively by the SSCos visiting the primary schools. However, one initial concern was the large amount of information for the primary school teachers, especially for those without a basic knowledge of the subject area.

Primary school meeting (Stage 3)

This stage involved each SSCo meeting with a PLT at a local primary school to present the OCM resource and explain the aims of the talent development research. Following some of the meetings, the PLTs were interviewed to obtain their perceptions and ideas.

Primary school teachers' perceptions

First impressions

Teachers appreciated a resource that featured moving images rather than the still images they had worked from previously. Another perceived benefit was the facility to enable viewing movement skills from different angles. Teachers found the software 'extremely easy to operate' and to navigate.

The dissemination process

It was suggested that this could be an effective 'two-way process' where teachers found it useful to interact with SSCos and discuss the potential uses of the resource:

'It's useful to bounce ideas off each other and just confirm possibly what you are thinking already . . . to act as a sounding board for each other.'

Advantages of the resource

Teachers felt that OCM could help them 'view talent' among their class groups and identify those who were physically able, but also encourage those with good performance analysis skills:

'. . . it could also be used by children. I could really imagine children looking at that video and being able to make critical comments without feeling that they were offending their peers.'

'Hotspots' were highlighted as a key feature of the resource to encourage pupils to focus on improving all parts of a movement skill with the help of an on-screen explanation that younger children could read and understand:

'I think it empowers the children because they are able to look at the hotspots and identify what they need to do to progress in that particular skill.'

Implementation (Stage 4)

This stage consisted of primary school teachers planning and delivering a PE lesson featuring OCM as a talent development strategy. Lesson observations were followed by semi-structured interviews with the teacher.

Case study of a primary school

The teacher in this study is a non-PE specialist. The Year 5 lesson he delivered was divided equally into two thirty-minute phases, the first of which was a classroom activity to discuss the movement skills associated with striking a tennis ball. The second half of the lesson was a practical activity in which the pupils applied the theory to physical practice. The teacher used the resource with an aim to identify pupils with both physical and cognitive ability.

Teacher's perceptions

First impressions

'Well I'm not a specialist PE teacher so I was looking at it from a lay-person's point of view basically, but I found it easy to install, easy to follow, the instructions were simple. I worked through it looking at the different sections and I found it very easy to understand and I hoped easy to use.'

Methods used

The SSCo and the teacher had worked together to prepare a medium-term plan featuring OCM within curricular PE lessons. The lessons were focused on specific movement skills and it was useful for the SSCo to benefit from the knowledge of a PE specialist:

'First of all, the use of the software was demonstrated to me by [SSCo's name] from [secondary school's name] and I observed that lesson when she demonstrated with my class. The following day, I used the software in exactly the same way that she'd used it with the parallel Year 5 class and I found it quite easy. It is very teacher friendly, that's the thing. Because I'm not a specialist, I needed help.'

Focusing on specific skills, the children became engaged in analysing movements and answering directed questions regarding the examples displayed on the interactive whiteboard. Analysing the videos enabled the pupils to develop their own performances in the practical phase of the lesson:

'What the children have seen on the video, they've developed in the PE lesson (practical). They've been able to remember the videos they've seen, the correct way that children have performed tasks and they've been able to emulate that.'

Most useful features

The printable resources were used to support the teacher's knowledge of the skills and increase confidence in explaining more technical points:

'... I've been able to print out tasks and skills that I need to develop. It means that I'm not teaching any misconceptions; I'm teaching it exactly as the CD shows it.'

OCM and talent identification

OCM was used by this teacher to help him identify pupils who were talented in different aspects of PE, as well as the physical performers:

'... they (the talented pupils) may be the ones who can pick out the faults and they may be able to relay that to their peers, they may be able to tell me that that's the problem. Then of course there are those in the playground and I can use it (OCM) because I can look how it's supposed to be done and then look at my children and say "that's good, that's spot on" ... so that's two ways which it will pick out the talented children; maybe those who are going to help and teach others and those who can actually do it.'

Other comments

It was considered to be an appropriate resource for Year 5 pupils when used in this way. Analysing the video clips developed the pupils' analysis skills and their own performances consequently benefited from an increased knowledge and understanding of the motor patterns. However, the teacher also believed that if it was applied to a younger age group, their improvements in performance might result in the skills being too basic for them when they reach Year 5. Therefore, to benefit further progress and skill development, a sequel CD aimed at a higher age group would be useful.

Evaluation meeting (Stage 5)

Following the seven-week trial of the resource, a meeting was organised for all SSCos and the PDM to discuss their experiences and evaluate the strategy.

Contacting the schools

Key points:

- initial contact often made with the PLT
- supportive approach: SSCos offered support if needed
- resource promotion: highlighting the positive elements of the resource, the potential and how it can aid teaching
- sports science approach: high-tech resource encouraging ICT skills
- lesson delivery: some SSCos delivered a PE lesson using the resource. This raised the SSCos' own awareness of the resource and also provided a useful demonstration for the teachers.

Methods

1. Talent identification: The teacher uses the resource to improve movement vocabulary (knowledge of movement skills) in order to identify talented pupils more effectively.
2. Talent enrichment: The teacher uses the resource during PE lessons to help explain the 'perfect model' of performance to talented pupils (direct use of resource or use of printed copies of materials).
3. Knowledge and understanding: The teacher allows the pupils to access the resource with aiming to develop knowledge and understanding of their own and others' movement skills.

Method 1 feedback:

- Primary school teachers welcomed the assistance.
- Primary school teachers appeared to be more concerned with improving the quality of PE for all pupils regardless of ability levels.
- Time-consuming to work from the CD – laminated printouts are more suitable for teacher reference during lessons.

Method 2 feedback:

- Provided a great introduction to the lesson. Provided a focus and generates pupil enthusiasm/interest.
- Resulted in great input and positive feedback from the pupils.
- It was easy to coach/teach from the points on the CD.

Method 3 feedback:

- This method was not as prevalent; SSCos felt that this strategy may become more effective in the long term.
- Many schools were still in the early stages of establishing talented cohorts and therefore deliberately focused on effective methods of identification.

Activity areas

SSCos felt that OCM was most effective in the following activity:

- athletics
- striking and fielding (rounders).

Most useful components of the resource

Now Make a Difference (NMAD) feature:

- useful for teaching points.

Hotspots:

- useful to have short phrases that explain everything
- breaks down the skill into the relevant components
- both pupils and teachers can relate to the teaching points.

Split screen:

- Pupils can identify weak performance from the on-screen demonstrations and avoid criticising their peers.
- Pupils are able to model the skills they see on screen very easily.
- The pupils relate to the examples of late motor patterns very well and this helps maintain a focus on the task.

Talent identification:

- SSCos expressed a need for criteria to identify talent: 'Are we identifying similar movements to the screen?'
- Older pupils found it easy to perform to the perfect model; therefore it was harder to identify (separate) the talented physical performers amongst older pupils. It was felt to be more relevant for the younger pupils if the aim was to identify physically talented pupils.

Talent provision:

- It was felt that initially the resource should be implemented for all and adapted as a talent development resource following longer-term provision.
- In terms of movement analysis, SSCos reported that the more able children felt that some of the early motor patterns were too obvious to highlight, whereas less able pupils identified more faults.
- More able pupils perhaps thought the task was to help younger pupils.
- It was perceived to be a useful resource for differentiating tasks and equipment according to ability levels, e.g. catching drills.

What would you do differently/recommendations?

- As an SSCo training activity, a practical example of a PE lesson featuring OCM would provide a useful indication of how the resource could be used.
- A resource specifically designed for SSCos would be useful, i.e. a pack containing more details and the role of the SSCos in the dissemination process.

- Focus on one of the methods/aims rather than including all within a single session.
- Suggestion that PDM should deliver the resource directly to the PLTs to ensure accuracy of information; which may be forgotten/altered as a result of multi-stage cascade process.
- Schools would welcome information on expectations/standards for the primary schools regarding good practice.
- The seven-week research period was not long enough to trial the strategy. More time would reveal the full potential and possibilities of using OCM to develop talent.

Additional comments:

- What would be helpful on the CD is more examples of later motor patterns for each skill. More than one example would allow pupils and teachers to identify common elements of good technique, e.g. three examples of a good throw.

Partnership development manager's feedback

Initial SSCo introduction to the resource resulted in a few concerns. However, once the SSCos were clear about the focus and the task, the feedback was generally very positive.

Installing the software was problematic in some cases:

- not all SSCos had a laptop computer
- not all SSCos had internet access via their laptops.

SSCo progress was monitored via telephone feedback and regular SSCo meetings. These meetings provided an opportunity to share thoughts and ideas and provide feedback regarding PLTs' perceptions, e.g. that the resource was ideal for developing the skills of less able pupils.

To facilitate the SSCo training, the PDM felt that it would be useful to present the CD within a realistic environment, i.e. within a practical PE lesson.

The next stage of the research and the Oakbank partnership involvement is to discuss intentions of future involvement at the next SSCo meeting; to establish whether the SSCos wish to remain involved and to what extent.

Summary and conclusions

The aim of the study was to provide a greater understanding of how OCM could be utilised as a talent development resource in primary school PE.

The five-stage dissemination process was successful in that 5 out of 6 SSCos set up strategies in at least one of their primary schools. Primary school teachers provided very positive feedback and appreciated the opportunity to work with SSCos and the OCM software. All teachers perceived the study to be beneficial to their work and were able to implement the resource as the research intended.

Teachers recognised the potential of OCM as a talent development strategy, particularly in identifying pupils with good analysis skills.

Of the three methods suggested, methods 1 and 2 were the most frequently used. Teachers believed that method 3 would become more prevalent once a talented group of pupils had been identified.

Resources

For a sample short-term plan see 'Observing Children Moving (Striking)' on the accompanying CD.

Talent identification portfolio (TIP)

Explanation

Following observation and formative assessment, an initial identification of talent is briefly recorded. The TIP is a means of recording the different types of evidence of talent. Schools can easily devise portfolios that match their specific situations. The TIP contains information on individual pupils' areas of talent in physical education.

Aim

The aim of the TIP is to allow for the initial identification of talent to be systematically recognised and recorded. Once identification details have been completed on the TIP the information can be used for moderation purposes across physical education teachers within a department.

Method

Recording of information relating to the nature of talent being identified can be conducted in accordance with the overall criteria found on the TIP without a specific area of focus. An alternative to this method is where the department agrees to focus on a particular ability, i.e. personal ability, and the TIP is used to highlight instances in which pupils have shown talent in this area.

Issues

To maintain the essence of rarity within the talent identification process TIPs should not be used for every pupil in a teaching group, but only for those pupils displaying ability over and above that of their peers.

It may be advisable in the first instance at departmental level to highlight an area of identification (e.g. identifying creativity) and work collectively to establish talented pupils within each teaching group and then meet collectively as a department to discuss outcomes of the process.

Resources

A TIP template is provided on the accompanying CD.

Revealing opportunities

Explanation

By 'revealing opportunities' we mean planning activities for focused observation and assessment; it forms a natural complement to the formative assessment and portfolio strategies described above.

Aim

The teacher could plan for revealing opportunities to allow for talent to emerge within an area of activity, a specific ability (e.g. leadership), a National Curriculum strand (e.g. acquiring and developing skills), or a specific sport.

Method

One way to do this is to include lesson objectives with specific focus upon those abilities that are not so easy to observe. For example, an objective could be added in order to identify personal ability, such as cooperating with and supporting others, whilst using essentially the original lesson content.

Example of the strategy in practice

Cardinal Heenan Sports College, Liverpool

Description

In this example, the teacher introduces a peer assessment task to a Year 8 tennis lesson. Stroke technique cards provide the pupils with teaching points and diagrams of the perfect model to illustrate the phases of the forehand and backhand stroke. Pupils work in small groups to analyse, record (using a template) and feedback information on the quality of each other's performance. This enables the teacher to observe skills beyond physical performance and reveals the pupils with high cognitive and interpersonal ability.

Teachers' views

The teachers at the school believe in maximising learning opportunities by providing a variety of stimuli to appeal to pupils' individual learning styles:

'Pupils can actually analyse their own technique . . . look at the breakdown of the skill . . . visually looking at what they are doing . . . using things like task cards . . . peer analysis.'

Teachers believe in developing pathways for pupils with good coaching skills as well as the performance pathways for the physically talented:

'Now one person might be fantastic at a forehand drive . . . but he might not be able to coach his peer, he might not have the knowledge and understanding of how to actually achieve the skill . . . the pupil who maybe can't perform as well, he can still achieve in the lesson and he can still improve his self-esteem. Pupils can be identified as good coaches, good role models. So not only can you talent identify the players maybe who'll go onto the clubs, we can feed pupils into JSLA programme, into the CSLA programme, keep them involved in the sports college link, so they can then teach our feeder primary schools.'

Resources

A sample 'revealing opportunities' short-term plan is provided on the accompanying CD.

> CHAPTER 4

Provision

In the previous section 'identification', a jargonised gifted and talented term, was equated with the more familiar teaching term of 'assessment'. Therefore, it is not surprising that the following section on 'provision' has explicit parallels with 'best practice' principles of teaching.

Strategies to facilitate the development of gifted and talented pupils must be designed within the context of a broader provision that meets the needs of all pupils. This provision needs to offer opportunities for everyone to experience challenge and to enable a continuous cycle of identification–provision–evaluation–identification to be maintained.

Enrichment and various forms of extension and acceleration within a differentiated approach form the core of the following sections of this chapter which outline key considerations in the provision for talented pupils in PE.

Enrichment

Recently Ofsted (2004) reported that whilst certain methods of provision for talented pupils in PE, such as mentoring, were effective; there remained a need to develop additional approaches that have mainstream curricular impact. Similarly, recent studies have found that the majority of strategies used to provide for talented pupils in PE existed in extracurricular settings, few of which had a direct impact on mainstream curricular experiences of the talented pupils in question (Bailey, Morley and Dismore, 2005; Tremere, Morley and Bailey, 2005).

Concerned with improving the quality of existing practices by challenging and stimulating talented pupils in ways that require innovative and imaginative responses; enrichment is one teaching and learning strategy that, if targeted at curricular practices, can ensure equity of access for all pupils and help create a sustained and supportive educational environment for talented pupils.

Principles of enrichment in PE

One of a number of underlying principles, Renzulli's (1977, quoted in Clark and Callow, 2002) enrichment triad model has been used in education internationally for over 25 years.

In many respects this approach facilitates the whole talent development process from identification through to provision and as such provides an excellent tool for assessing potential outside of other structured identification systems. An example of how this three-tiered model could be used in a PE lesson to effectively challenge talented pupils is given below.

Type 1 enrichment

At this level, pupils are captivated by either the task they are being asked to perform or its theme. Providing a wide range of activities from which to choose will facilitate more wide-scale engagement. For example, in a dance based around the theme of a circus pupils would be asked to list the sights and the sounds of a circus and imitate the movements of various performers. Activities could be stimulated by props and task cards but would remain within the structured time of the lesson. At this stage recognition of high abilities and interests would be noted for future development.

Type 2 enrichment

Pupils now require specific skills to pursue their level of understanding more effectively. Dance skills integral to motif development such as individual reflection, the enlargement of moves and change of speed could lead onto canon, unison and mirror to act as a foundation for experimentation when composing a dance. Use of beats with instruments or clapping can be presented within groups to allow the group to develop and create a dance. Group work forms the basis of this level and tasks which extend beyond the dance studio or gym are used to meet the needs of identified groups, and individuals within groups, who require challenging in different ways. Therefore, it may also be necessary to incorporate the teaching of skills necessary to pursue group work outside the curriculum.

Type 3 enrichment

Groups now formalise their interest in a particular piece of work, perhaps from designing a section of a dance, i.e. 'the dance of the clowns', to the production of the whole show involving all of the collective dances within the teaching group. Some talented pupils will feel adequately equipped following their experiences at Type 1 and Type 2 activities to continue this project work in their own time.

This approach suits the multidimensional aspect of talent development in physical education as it allows pupils to fulfil a variety of roles within a common task.

Differentiated practices

Differentiation is not only at the heart of inclusive and effective teaching but it is also a central feature of provision for talented pupils in PE. The following diagram explains a model of differentiation that has been refined and developed to advance the traditional 'outcome' and 'task' based differentiation approach, and in doing so presents an excellent vehicle for explaining the potential for differentiated talent development practices.

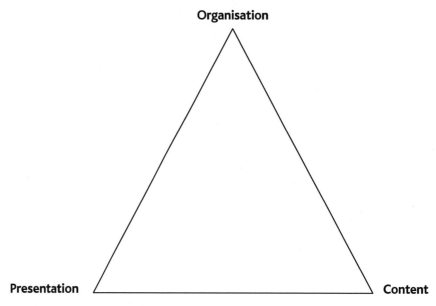

A model of differentiation for enriching provision (from Bailey, 2001)

Through this model we can begin to map out some of the underlying principles of provision for talented pupils in PE and sport.

Differentiation by organisation

Grouping

Talented pupils like working with pupils of similar abilities; it gives them opportunities to operate at a high level and extends their boundaries and expectations of themselves and others. In mixed ability groups this causes problems when attempting to establish differentiated practices that challenge every individual within the group according to their needs. When teaching mixed ability groups there may be a tendency to pitch the level of the lesson at the mean, the middle and the mass in order to fulfil expectations of the National Curriculum and this has obvious implications for the talented pupil who remains unchallenged.

As to the proven benefits of different approaches to grouping, national and international research is mixed. Some researchers suggest that average ability pupils benefited most from mixed ability grouping and talented pupils from ability specific grouping, whilst others report that benefits gained from within a streamed group for the highly able are more significant than indicators of self-esteem for being part of the group (Freeman, 1998).

Within mixed ability groups there may be a tendency to use talented pupils to coach their less able peers. In this role it is likely that the talented pupil will inevitably improve their social and personal ability but there is a danger if overused that such an approach may be detrimental to their own personal knowledge, skills and understanding. Mixed ability groups are actually in decline in education per se but physical education is one of a few subjects that retains this grouping mechanism (Benn and Chitty, 1996). The debate on mixing, setting (using ability in a specific subject) and streaming (using overall ability) pupils into groups has been in existence practically since education began and is outside the scope of this book. What is relevant to the teacher here is to understand the reasons for grouping in certain ways in terms of how organisational systems can effectively enhance provision for talented pupils.

The following table is split into year- and class-based grouping systems and represents an understanding of some of the key considerations when grouping pupils.

Year- and class-based grouping systems

Grouping system	Advantages	Disadvantages
Year-based		
Mixed ability	• Talented pupils can be used to demonstrate and coach less able pupils	• Employing a range of practices to suit a wide range of needs is difficult • Level of delivery is often aimed at children with average ability
Streaming (most commonly with an emphasis on ability in English, maths, science)	• Lessons can concentrate on the cognitive dimensions of the subject area and prepare for examination PE more effectively	• Although PE provides for pupils with high academic ability, abilities other than those recognised within academic subjects will not be used as primary indicators of talent.
Setting by subject area	• Assessing level of appropriate tasks and challenge is easier and pupils work at an appropriate pace for their own needs	• Generally based on current performance and therefore limited in recognising potential • Some baseline indicators of talent may only cover certain activity areas • Potential for negative 'labelling' effect on talented group and lower sets
Setting by a single or limited number of specific activity areas (e.g. games activities)	• Within the specified activity area talented pupils have the opportunity to work with other pupils of similar ability	• When the curriculum changes to other activity areas than the one used to initially group pupils, the levels of ability within the group are wide ranging
Class-based		
Friendship groups	• Pupils are more likely to understand the strengths and weaknesses of others within their group	• Potential for talented pupils to become distracted and stray from the task
Randomly selected groups	• Allows opportunities for talented pupils to develop as effective communicators and readily adopt roles in unfamiliar environments	• Does not allow for selection by ability and therefore raises issues related to appropriate challenge for all pupils within the group
Ability groups	• Differentiated practices and tasks can be targeted more specifically at certain groups • Certain aspects of the same task can be emphasised to provide more effectively for certain abilities (e.g. those with high levels of creativity)	• There is potential for lower ability groups to be 'left behind' and this may have implications if re-integration is to be considered

Space

The use of space within physical activity environments is often driven by consideration of the factors of time and pressure. For example, in games activities, it is generally recognised that a decrease in the amount of space a child has to operate within would normally be associated with an increase in pressure on the performance of the skill or movement. Therefore, to create the right level of challenge, space is a critical factor in regulating the opportunities for success at an appropriate level for the child. In some instances the use of more or less space may stimulate innovative thought and would therefore be suitable for children with high levels of creativity.

Roles

The potential for the overuse of certain roles in the provision for talented pupils, most notably that of coach or demonstrator, has already been mentioned. In effect, just because a pupil can perform outstandingly well in a specific area may not provide grounds for suggesting they are competent at, or comfortable with, coaching their peers. However, the use of a variety of roles does have a place within talent development in PE and the talented pupils with high levels of social ability in particular will thrive in the role of evaluator, leader, coach and manager.

Presentation

Teaching style

The use of a particular teaching style will have an enormous impact on the potential of children with a wide range of abilities to access high quality learning experiences. Mosston and Ashworth (1986) developed a teaching spectrum which maps out teaching styles ranging from command style to discovery. The table opposite represents an adaptation of the teaching styles offered by Mosston and Ashworth and suggests some implications for their use with talented pupils.

If provision is to meet the needs of all pupils, the teaching styles used must challenge the specific ability of the identified pupil across the range of National Curriculum activity areas. Of course, recognising the multidimensional aspect of talent identification means that a range of abilities are likely to be unearthed. This may require a number of teaching styles being employed within the same lesson for different groups of pupils, within certain sections of the lesson, or at various points within the scheme of work.

Response

As well as confirming pupils' understanding of key aspects of the lesson related to knowledge, understanding and application, children's responses should also determine subsequent content and teaching styles. Crucial to the ongoing development of provision, the key to success here is to elicit response in a variety of ways to ensure the preferred learning and thinking styles of each child are catered for. In PE this can take the form of an ongoing dialogue of questions and answers, demonstration, group discussion and verbal feedback within analysis of performance.

Implications for using particular teaching styles with talented pupils

Teaching style	Explanation	Implications for use with talented pupils
A **Command**	Occasionally also referred to as a 'didactic' style of teaching; the teacher makes all of the decisions related to the activity as to what, where, when and how.	Pupils with high levels of physical ability are likely to excel in response to this style as it can be used to maximise the knowledge and performance base. While perhaps maximising performance product, this style of teaching suppresses creativity and inhibits the understanding of processes involved in the acquisition of knowledge and skills.
B **Practice**	Teacher makes decisions before and after the activity with learner making decisions during the task. Teacher determines parameters of learning.	Pupils with high levels of cognitive ability will begin to prosper in this environment as information processed from doing the activity can be used to determine actions in subsequent tasks.
C **Reciprocal**	Pupils are asked to evaluate a partner's performance using set criteria within roles of observer and doer with opportunities for role reversal. Teacher determines set criteria for performance and supports pupils where necessary.	As well as continuing to facilitate quality experiences for pupils with high levels of physical and cognitive abilities, pupils with high levels of social ability should encounter appropriate provision here as they are asked to communicate effectively with their peers and recognise strengths and areas of development.
D **Self-check**	Similar to teaching styles B & C in that teachers will establish the learning parameters although skills learnt in C are now used to focus on learners' own improvement according to set criteria.	This style is useful for a range of abilities as self-regulation is an inherent characteristic of talented pupils. Pupils with high levels of personal ability will develop effectively in this environment as they will generally have high levels of self-esteem and relish the opportunity to build upon their strengths.
E **Inclusion**	A differentiated approach to teaching whereby multiple levels of performance exist in the same task allowing the pupils to determine their own entry level into the activity.	In many respects this bears similarities to the previously mentioned 'triad enrichment model'. As the level of challenge is appropriate to the needs of individuals, and they are responsible for accessing the provision at their own level, this should afford talented pupils of all abilities opportunities for success. The nature and scope of the core task will determine the successful inclusion of talented pupils.
F **Discovery**	Whereas teaching styles A to E rely on memory recall and associated cognitive processes the discovery style engages the learner in the production of ideas and discovery of concepts. Allowing the learner the opportunities to develop and apply different ideas is fundamental in this style of teaching.	Pupils with high levels of creativity will flourish in this environment as they begin to flex their minds to the range of options available in response to the stimulus provided by the teacher. Some talented pupils with high levels of physical ability who have relatively low levels of creativity may prefer more structured environments and become frustrated with the lack of direction.
G **Guided discovery**	The teacher asks questions to lead pupils into specific areas of discovery.	As a result of the implications for using a discovery teaching style mentioned above, this style may be more suitable for teachers to challenge pupils with high levels of physical ability in a slightly more structured manner than F. This should then allow them to experiment with previously learned information and skills outside of their usual comfort zone.
H **Divergent style**	This teaching style requires teachers to design problems that elicit a series of alternative solutions.	For pupils with high levels of cognitive and creative ability this environment is extremely productive. Whereas previously pupils responded in different ways using previously acquired skills and information now diversity of thought is the key.

In general educational terms, Gardner's (1983) theory of multiple intelligences (linguistic, kinaesthetic etc.) has been used to classify a range of intelligences pupils may possess that would then begin to signify the ways in which they would prefer to be challenged. Although this may begin the process of identifying learning styles, one way of being more specific about the ways in which we present information to pupils, and we expect them to present information to us, is in terms of their thinking styles. One approach to thinking about thinking originates from the psychological system known as neuro-linguistic programming (or NLP, for short). NLP speaks about thinking – or information processing – as reproducing in the mind the sensory components of what we see, hear, smell, taste and touch with our senses (O'Connor and Seymour, 2003). These are known as the representational systems, or the VAK systems, and these stand for the way by which we represent information: visual (eyes) – for the pictures, sights, images; auditory (ears) – for the sounds, noises, tones; kinaesthetic (body) – for the sensations, feelings, touch. When we think about something, anything, we encode our thoughts using our senses. This approach has the great virtue of making our talk about students' thinking much more specific, and it also offers an exciting way to be much more focused in the way we present information to our pupils. The VAK approach to recognising thinking styles enhances the opportunities for pupils to excel in their preferred domain and also stimulates curiosity and engagement in the subject matter. Some examples of how responses can be elicited using the VAK approach are mentioned below.

'Visual' thinker responses:

- using a photograph or diagram of the 'perfect model', observe demonstrations and feedback in comparison to the picture

- demonstrate acquisition of key technical points through repeating a specific movement or skill as presented by the teacher

- within the planning of a sequence, draw a diagram or picture representing the movements associated with the sequence as an overview of the whole sequence or moves performed by individuals in isolation.

'Auditory' thinker responses:

- describe the sound of the correct movement, e.g. the 'thwack' of the racquet for an overhead clear in badminton or the 'silence' of the push pass in hockey

- verbally explain the reason why teams perform well in certain situations and why certain members of the group play important individual roles in achieving a common goal

- use auditory stimulus (music, instruments, clapping, noises) to create responses through movement (not confined to dance activities here, this works equally well within most activities, e.g. teaching the patterns of movement for the lay-up in basketball or the steps in the triple jump).

'Kinaesthetic' thinker responses:

- use metaphors and analogies to describe the movement, e.g. the preparation for the overhead clear feels like 'scrubbing your back with a brush in the shower', or 'look through the window' in preparation for the bowling action in cricket or perhaps performing a dance in unison feels like 'dominoes falling over'

- improve somebody else's performance by describing the 'feeling' of performing a particular movement

- explain correct movement whilst performing the action in a 'walk through, talk through' approach.

Questioning

Many of the above responses may require some form of subsequent questioning to allow pupils the opportunity to elaborate on their initial thoughts or movements and also to gauge their depth of learning. Open-ended questions that stimulate thinking and concentrate on process as much as product are particularly useful here, as are those that arouse curiosity through the use of probing questions; using 'why?' as a precursor to a question is as important as the question of 'how?' So, in general:

1. Questioning of pupils should form an integral part of the planning, teaching and evaluative processes involved in an activity.

2. Ask the pupils for their understanding of specific terminology and acronyms. As an example, it is amazing how many pupils there are that don't understand what the initials PE actually stand for!

3. Ask questions which allow pupils to justify their actions or summary of events.

4. Ask the question to the whole group, and then:

   a. select an individual to respond

   b. ask the group to get into pairs and formulate the possibilities of an answer within a set time, self-nominate one of the pair to respond

   c. allow them the opportunity to verbalise, demonstrate, draw, mind map, brainstorm, discuss, and experiment with, their response.

5. Give the group the answer(s) and get them to think of the question.

6. Don't always allow pupils to raise their hands. At times this is simply showing us that the pupil knows the answer and simultaneously allows the rest of the group to 'switch off'. Whilst eliciting their response is important it may be more prudent to engage other members of the group in offering an answer.

7. Accept all responses; they may not be wholly correct and appropriate for the direction you have chosen but allow the pupils' learning needs to direct the focus rather than the content.

8. When questioning in a large group pay attention to the 'polar points'; those pupils located at the extreme ends of the group and those at the back.

9. Some talented pupils may not always want to be the centre of attention. Ascertain which pupils are more comfortable at providing responses in whole group, small group and individual situations.

Resources

Provision for talent development in physical education can be significantly enhanced through the use of appropriate resources. While the availability of ICT resources has allowed some teachers the opportunity to experiment with a range of delivery tools, there still remains a need for teachers to assess the educational virtues of selecting certain resources to support teaching and learning.

Resource implication criteria

- Is the resource appropriate for the developmental ability of the group/talented pupil?
- How will the learning of pupils be enhanced through the use of the resource?
- Do the pupils need preparing for the effective use of the resource?
- Is the amount of time spent in familiarising the children with the resource in proportion to the educational benefits gained?
- Are there alternative resources that will produce a similar outcome?

Differentiation by content

Pace and acceleration

As talented pupils will more often than not progress through a series of tasks at a faster rate than their peers, it may be appropriate to consider the most suitable level and amount of content necessary to challenge them effectively.

When considering the notion of suitable content to match the individual's needs 'more' may not always be better. In this regard it may seem appropriate to accelerate talented pupils' learning by using material from later Key Stages of the National Curriculum or indeed by allowing them to access the different levels of examination PE early. Whilst this may be appropriate for some pupils, the increase in the pace of delivery in this way presents a danger that provision will lack depth leaving higher order thinking skills underdeveloped (Eyre, 2001). This sort of 'content acceleration' has been viewed sceptically in other quarters, in so far as it is considered that the quality of learning experiences through enrichment should always be used as the primary vehicle of delivery (Hymer and Michel, 2002).

As already discussed to some extent in the section on mixed ability, where some children are working at levels significantly beyond that of their peers the organisation of curricular content, both within a single lesson and over a period of time, can become problematic. The pace of delivery is another important aspect of ensuring quality provision for talented pupils; if the pace is too fast and pupils experience limited success, pupils may become frustrated and anxious about their lack of progression. Conversely, if the pace is too slow pupils may become bored and restless and it is this type of environment which could cause talented pupils to become disaffected from the subject area. The model below represents the relationship between the level of challenge set and the possible implications for pupils with different levels of ability. The target zone in this particular example is where pupils are in their 'flow'.

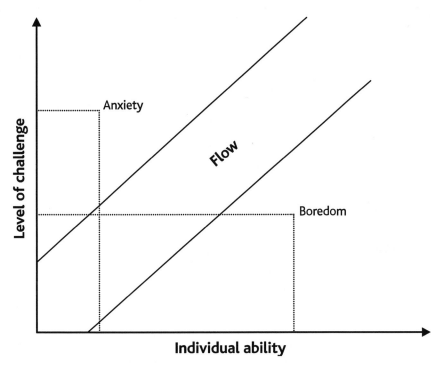

Matching abilities and challenges (from Csikszentmihalyi, 1975)

Level

The ability of talented pupils to complete tasks at more refined levels consistently means that consideration of desirable outcomes is essential in ensuring they reach a productivity level appropriate to their ability. In some cases this may mean that lesson objectives presented to the group at the start of the lesson make explicit reference to expectations of pupils operating at high levels of competency across a range of abilities. Examples of possible learning outcomes for talented pupils are given on the next page.

Learning outcomes for talented pupils in PE

- Express the same answer to a question in as many different ways as possible.
- Understand the use of periodisation in a training programme across a range of sports.
- Use movements acquired in previous lessons in an unfamiliar environment.
- Select other pupils' interpretations of a tactic or compositional idea to enhance your own individual or team's performance.
- Use information gleaned from consulting a range of sources to lead a team effectively.
- Cooperate effectively in group situations whilst adopting a variety of roles.
- Understand and apply concepts of precision, control and fluency in increasingly demanding situations as determined by the pupil.
- Explore methods of communication in a range of situations and measure the effectiveness of the methods observed or adopted.
- Provide a number of alternatives to a single solution and assess the suitability of each alternative in the production of a task.
- Demonstrate leadership skills in a range of situations displaying appropriate flexibility of approach.
- Create a game where principles of depth, width and mobility can be used to assess its success.
- Analyse the most effective method of giving feedback to a performer.
- Recognise own strengths and areas for development and formulate an action plan for progression.
- Formulate methods of assessing your peers effectively in a range of activities.
- Assess the progression of a project in relation to its outcomes.

The strategic approach outlined in the previous chapter seems to us the most effective way of galvanising the intricacies of the school environment, the needs of the child and the expertise and aspirations of teachers. In a similar vein strategies for providing for talented pupils are outlined here in the same form as those for identification.

Celebrating achievement

Explanation

This strategy aims to provide talented pupils with positive reinforcement for their efforts and success in PE and school sport. Notice boards can be used to display the latest news, and school internet sites could feature articles on pupils' achievements. The school colours award is another common strategy used in schools whereby pupils achieve different colours (represented with school ties, badges etc.) according to their level of representation in sports and activities. The representative honours strategy aims to encourage talented pupils to strive for success whilst raising teachers' awareness of pupils' interests and commitments, often outside of school hours.

Example of the strategy in practice

Lymm High School, Cheshire

Description

The 'Honours Programme' aimed to achieve consistency in the award of school colours across the different halls at the school. School colours up to county level are awarded to pupils by the heads of hall and full colours are awarded by the head teacher for achieving regional or national level sport. The strategy was developed to award recognition for all successful sports performers.

Teachers' views

The teachers felt that the strategy encouraged more pupils to attend after-school sports clubs and had a positive effect on PE lessons in the schools:

'The more we get going to sports clubs, hopefully the more their attitude is positive within PE lessons . . . they're the role models . . . you've got more kids who are proactive. We tend to find that those who achieve in sport, also achieve in PE.'

The programme was considered to raise the self-esteem of those awarded with school honours:

'I think it gives them a bit of a buzz and prestige . . . that they wouldn't necessarily get in school.'

Resources

For a sample school honours programme see Appendix 4.1 (also on the CD).

Differentiation

As discussed in detail earlier in this chapter, by setting relevant challenges and goals, this strategy aims to provide an appropriate level of challenge for all pupils within a mixed ability group.

Example of the strategy in practice

The case study explored the use of differentiation in curricular PE as a talent development strategy across all activity areas. The PE department implement a multi-method approach featuring the following methods of differentiation:

- **By task** – to enable pupils with high levels of physical ability to attempt more complex movements and routines.
- **By role** – talented pupils are encouraged to deliver aspects of the lesson such as warm-up activities to the rest of the group. This helps to develop their understanding of the task and also their interpersonal skills.
- **By activity equipment** – where relevant, the talented pupils have access to a broader range of equipment in order to challenge and develop their skills.

Teachers' views

Differentiation challenges the talented pupils in the group but also provides beneficial role models for the other pupils in the group:

'If you ask them to teach something, they have to break it down (the movement pattern) . . . They are thinking about how they actually do the skill before they teach it to the other groups.'

Resources

For a sample short-term plan see 'Differentiation for talented pupils' on the CD.

Extension tasks

The employment of extension tasks within lessons is an essential tool in ensuring an enriched environment for talented pupils. QCA schemes of work (QCA/DFEE, 2000) provide an insight into a range of viable extension tasks, which may be incorporated into any lesson plan, regardless of level of ability, age or activity area. Examples of these are worksheets, off-site visits and the use of the internet to develop the acquisition of a range of advanced skills.

Resources

A sample short-term plan with extension tasks is provided on the CD.

Fundamental movement skills

Example of the strategy in practice (1)

Newsome Sports College Partnership, Huddersfield

Description

The school has set up a 'Fundamental Movement Skills' club for talented Year 5 and 6 pupils from local schools within the sports college partnership. Approximately 20 pupils meet once a week after school to participate in activities designed to develop the generic aspects of movement such as agility, speed and coordination. During the eight week scheme, pupils learn how fundamental movement skills can be applied to a variety of sports and games. On completion of the scheme, pupils and parents/carers are provided with information regarding local clubs and facilities to encourage out-of-school participation in sports and physical activities.

Teachers' views

The partnership development manager (PDM) at Newsome Sports College believes that children tend to specialise in certain sports too early. She explained that the aim of the club is to help the pupils develop a diverse range of fundamental skills that are relevant to a variety of sports. As the programme progresses, the pupils start to see how these skills are useful and they understand the transfer of certain skills between sports. As well as observing improvement in motor skills, the pupils also appear to gain confidence from the activities.

Pupils' views

The pupils perceived many benefits from attending the club and many felt that the club helped them improve at the sports they already played. They provided relevant examples from situations in sport to explain how fundamental skills could be applied. The pupils felt privileged to be part of a selected group and explained that their families were proud of them for being identified as talented. Some pupils said that their primary school teachers were interested in the types of activities they did at the club. For example, pupils from one school explained that during their PE lessons, their teacher would ask them to describe and demonstrate the skills they had learned.

Resources

A sample short-term plan with extension tasks is provided on the CD.

Example of the strategy in practice (2)

St Mary's Sports College, Hull

Description

The school has set up a 'High Performance Club' for talented pupils in Year 8 at the school who are invited to attend the club following a selection process based on their current performance levels in sport and achievements in physical education.

The strategy at this school is to adopt a generic skill approach that progresses from the fundamental stage of movement development to the 'training to train' phase suggested in the model of long-term athlete development (Balyi and Hamilton, 2000). The aim of the club is to provide the pupils with experience of a diverse range of activities and skills to enable more informed choices before specialising in certain sports. The sessions focus on different areas of motor development such as balance, coordination, reaction time, kinaesthetic awareness, speed, strength and agility.

A total of 31 sport and activity based sessions that focus on different areas of motor development are delivered lasting for one hour after school each week. The school has plans to set up similar high performance clubs for other year groups.

Teachers' views

'We noticed that there were some very able pupils and we basically wanted to extend and give them the opportunity to improve their skills.'

The teachers were familiar with the model of long-term athlete development and recognised that there was a lack of provision for pupils of that age at the 'learning to train' phase:

'We didn't think that any of the existing clubs in the school allowed us to build on those fundamental skills so we thought that there was a bit of a gap there and hence we wanted to set up a club which really addressed those skills.'

The club has been beneficial for the pupils in many ways:

'Because they are seen to be high performers, when it comes to their core PE lessons and also around school they're seen as leaders and leadership is a common theme we've got running through our curriculum . . . so from a social point of view I think it's very beneficial as well as developing them physically as well.'

The teachers were sensitive to certain issues associated with early specialisation in a single sport and encouraged the pupils to experience a range of activities:

'You always come across some students . . . they reach the age of maybe 14, 15, 16 and become disillusioned and because they've been so involved in maybe one sport to quite a high level they kind of drop out of sport altogether and it was addressing that as well.'

The teachers at the school believe that developing talent and creating sports pathways is important for not only the pupils and the school but also the local community:

'You look at now the effect of the stadium (Hull's new sports stadium) . . . the football club and the rugby club are doing well and I think the effect that has on the city is enormous and I think that's why talent is important . . . it raises people's expectations and it gives them a vision and like I say, in a place like Hull that's very very important.'

Pupils' views

The pupils explained how the club had helped them in PE and with their own sports:

'It helps with your PE skills, you learn how to coach . . . you learn a lot of skills for other sports, and in PE, sometimes they let us lead the warm-ups . . . people who go to "High Performance" lead the warm-ups for everybody else.'

Some pupils believed that the opportunity to coach others in core PE lessons had encouraged them to think about the principles of the skills:

'It develops your skills of thinking, you become more aware of things . . . you concentrate more.'

Pupils enjoyed attending the activities and appreciated the opportunity to be involved in the High Performance Club:

'I feel proud as well but also quite privileged to come to these extra sport lessons.'

Resources

For a sample short-term plan see 'High Performance Club' on the CD.

External coaching

There is a wealth of coaching expertise available to supplement existing sports practice in schools and the number of sports clubs seeking to develop partnerships with schools seems to be on the increase. Qualified coaches visiting schools can offer a different approach to the delivery of an activity and the introduction of a new face has the potential to enhance enthusiasm and motivation. The use of a coach within curricular and extracurricular time can also reinforce existing pathways through recognised sports routes.

Awards and courses

- Community Sports Leaders Award (CSLA)
- Junior Sports Leaders Award (JSLA)
- Sport for Life
- YMCS Fitness award
- activity leaders awards

The development of nationally recognised courses, such as CSLA, JSLA, and the more recent addition of web-based resources (e.g., 'Sport for Life', www. sportforlife.net) form a concurrent tier of accreditation.

GCSE taster lessons

Antipathy amongst girls, particularly within Key Stage 4 (Kay, 1995), has led to the investigation of more diverse, non-games-orientated approaches to motivate young girls and raise their aspirations to continue with sport once they leave school. One possible approach to addressing the antipathy of talented girls is increased enrolment onto examinable physical education courses, and 'taster' lessons could be used to ensure motivation is maintained.

CHAPTER 5

Support for learning

Talent – nature or nurture

[In the film The African Queen,] Katharine Hepburn, playing a missionary, pours Humphrey Bogart's gin into the river, and a discussion about Bogart's vulnerability to temptation ensues. 'But Missy,' he protests, 'it's just human nature.' 'Nature,' replies Hepburn, 'is what we are put into this world to rise above.'

(Kohn, 1995)

Probably the most frequently discussed topics in talent development relate, in one way or another, to the relative importance of biological and social contributions to high ability. Of course, it is not just academics who are interested in these issues. How are these top players so good? Is it the outcome of hard work and good coaching, or are they just born that way? Is it nurture or nature?

Two extreme responses to questions like this are called environmental and genetic determinism. Environmental determinists believe that people come into the world as blank slates and everything they become is due to experience and learning (Pinker, 2002). According to this view, our most talented students are those who have benefited from the most supportive parents, the best coaching and the most encouraging social settings. Genetic environmentalists, on the other hand, argue that our futures are written in our genes, in our biological makeup. Talented students, from this perspective, are simply born more able than their peers, and their success in the area of their talent is somewhat inevitable.

It may still be possible to find some representatives of these two extreme positions, but the great majority of informed people – almost everyone, in fact – fall somewhere in between these views. So, whilst some people might emphasise the importance of our biology, and others will stress environmental factors, almost all will acknowledge that high ability is the result of an interaction of biological and environmental influences, of nature and nurture, and they would find it difficult to separate the two. This view is nicely captured by Kimble (1993: 13–14), when he wrote, 'asking whether individual differences in behaviour are determined by heredity or environment is like asking whether the areas of rectangles are determined by their height or width'.

Nevertheless, it can be very difficult to give up totally simple either-or classifications. For example, guidance for teachers abounds with descriptions of personal characteristics of children with gifts and talents. The empirical basis for such lists is unclear, and their main function seems to be restricted to representing a 'template' of a gifted or talented child against which teachers can rank their students. For the present purposes, such descriptions are of limited value, since they rarely include reference to the types of abilities developed within physical education lessons. A more fruitful source of information is the type of longitudinal and psycho-biographical research discussed above. These studies suggest a range of differences between individuals' achievement that seem to form important conditions for high-level performance in various domains.

Historically, sport science research has emphasized the role of kinanthropometric and physical measures for the identification of individuals who have the potential to excel in a particular sport. According to this approach, sports talent can be successfully identified by searching for young people whose physiques and proportions match profiles of elite performers, a view summarized neatly by Grabiner and McKelvain (1987: 121): 'the ability to identify young people whose profile is consistent with that of elite gymnasts may enhance the sport development of the individual by giving information about future success'. Despite its intuitive appeal, this approach is flawed when working with young sports players for a number of reasons, including the facts that kinanthropometric and physical measures are unstable during adolescence and determinants of performance vary with growth, maturation and development (Abbott *et al.*, 2002).

This is not to deny the contribution of biological factors towards performance in any domain. The literature testifying to the hereditary nature of many cognitive and physiological characteristics is impressive (cf. Rankinen *et al.*, 2002). Research suggests that a range of factors that are likely to impact on performance in physical education contexts are genetically constrained, including sub-maximal aerobic capacity, resting heart rate, information processing and an individual's response to training. As compelling as this research is, however, there are a number of reasons for remaining tentative in the use and acceptance of genetic research data in the current area of study. Little genetic research has specifically examined elite performers, focusing instead on the general population, so it is inadvisable to assume too much from these findings. Also, the limited research that has explored the genetics of elite performers has been concerned with a narrow range of (relatively easily measurable) cognitive skills and physical measures, rather the multi-domain actions and procedures that are characteristic of physical education settings.

An adequate understanding of talent in physical education can only be gained by considering both the environmental and the personal characteristics that underlie such ability.

Environmental characteristics

Many children exhibiting signs of high ability during early childhood do not achieve high levels of performance in later life (Tannenbaum, 1983). Whilst there is a host of developmental and maturational factors that are likely to influence the development of ability during the childhood years (Abbott *et al.*, 2002), it also seems likely that a significant number of children never fulfil their early promise due to an inadequate or inappropriate social environment (Perleth *et al.*, 2000). Of course, there is no way of calculating the number of potentially talented children who were born and brought up in non-supportive backgrounds and whose gifts were never realised, but we might presume that figure to be high.

One aspect of the talented child's environment that has witnessed a considerable amount of research from a wide variety of domains is the family, and this includes some useful studies focusing on the influence of the family on the emergence of sporting talent (for example, Côté, 1999; Holt and Morley, 2004; Kay, 1995). In his study of 120 musicians, artists, athletes, mathematicians and scientists, Bloom (1985: 3) found 'strong evidence that no matter what the initial characteristics (or gifts) of the individuals, unless there is a long and intensive process of encouragement, nurturance, education and training, the individuals will not attain extreme levels of capability in these particular fields'.

Simonton (1998), through his psycho-biographical studies of world-class achievers, has argued that there is no ideal family for producing giftedness (see also Freeman, 2001), and the backgrounds of such individuals is, indeed, varied. However, certain patterns do emerge from the literature that suggest there are some family characteristics that are facilitative of the development of high ability in a specific area. So, children are more likely to realise their potential talent if they match some of the following (based on Bailey and Morley, forthcoming):

- parents achieved high standards in domain

- relatively high socioeconomic status

- ability and willingness to financially support participation and specialist support

- ability and willingness to invest high amounts of time to support the child's engagement in the activity

- parents are car owners

- relatively small family size

- two-parent family

- attendance at independent school.

As Kay (1995: 151) summarises, within the context of elite sport, 'children are simply much more likely to achieve success if they come from a certain type of family'.

A considerable amount of academic research has been carried out that examines the relationship between peer influence and participation in specific activities. Friendship seems to play a particularly significant role in decisions to invest time and effort in sports, compared with other domains. For example, Abernethy *et al.* (2002) reported that, in the early stages of their careers, the Australian elite athletes in their sample all mentioned having a group of friends who were also involved in sport. Research in other areas presents the relationship between high ability and peer influence as problematic. There is some evidence that the possession of a gift or talent can endanger social acceptance, and this seems to be especially the case for girls (Winner, 1996).

It seems tautologous to claim that schools influence the development of talent in physical education: by its nature, physical education is a school-based activity. Nevertheless, it would be remiss to overlook the contribution that schools make, since the outcomes of the talent development process are diverse and not restricted to educational aims. Formal schooling certainly seems to be an important factor in children's cognitive and academic development (Ceci, 1991). Moreover, the initial acquisition of culturally valued skills is most likely to occur during formal schooling. It is interesting to note, then, that elite adult performers in some domains, especially art and music, are often suspicious of formal education, believing such teaching to be unnecessary for the development of an individual's talent, and potentially destructive of their talent (Gardner, 1980). For example, none of the elite sculptors interviewed by Sloane and Sosniak (1985) had anything good to say about either their primary or secondary art education. These individuals attributed far greater influence to private teachers and professional artists.

The limited autobiographical evidence available suggests that elite sports players are much more positive about their school experiences, with numerous high-level athletes and sports players, like Martin Johnson, Sir Stephen Redgrave and Sally Gunnell, crediting school physical education teachers with identifying and then nurturing their talents (Johnson, 2003; Redgrave, 2000; Gunnell, 1995). However, whilst responsive and supportive physical education teachers constituted a necessary factor in the development of elite sports participation, they are rarely sufficient. Jean Côté and his colleagues (2003) cite specialist coaches as one of the main sources of influence on children as they progress through their development in sport. In the early stages, the coach's role is generally supplementary to that of school teachers, offering structured practice activities and emphasising basic skill development (Abernethy *et al.*, 2002). Only later (at approximately 13 years of age, in Abernethy's study) did the coach–athlete relationship become closer and more professional (Rowley, 1992).

Personal characteristics

One popular area of research with regard to elite performance is that which relates to their personal, psychological characteristics. Studies from a range of fields have established such characteristics as vital to high level performance

(Moore *et al.*, 1998; Bloom, 1985). As John Kane (1986: 191) put it: 'the ultimate factors accounting for achievement are likely to be the unique personal and behavioural dispositions which the individual brings to the actual performance.' Considering the role already attributed to practice in skill development, it is not surprising that aptitudes facilitative of many hours of training have been associated with exceptional achievement. So, determination and persistence in pursuing one's ambition has been identified as a factor, as has self-efficacy, ambition and autonomy. Motivation is a concept that underpins much of the literature on personal characteristics and numerous authors have attested to its central role in the development of talent in all domains (Sternberg, 2000; Renzulli, 1986).

Within the contexts of physical education and sporting activities, the role of fundamental movement skills may also be important. The specialised movements of different activities are built on a foundation of basic skills, such as running, jumping, balancing and turning (Bailey, 2000). Children who lack these basic skills 'are often relegated to a life of exclusion from organised and free play experiences of their peers, and subsequently, to a lifetime of inactivity because of their frustration in early movement behaviour' (Seefeldt *et al.*, cited in Abbott *et al.*, 2002: 19). Whilst it is difficult to envisage a causative relationship, and there is little empirical work in this area to date, it seems unarguable that high level performance in any formalised physical activity will be impossible without an adequate foundation of fundamental movement skills (Moore *et al.*, 1998).

Mentoring

Mentoring has no universally agreed definition, as is clearly indicated in a large amount of the literature on the subject (Stephenson and Taylor, 1995, Wright and Smith, 2000). This is partly due to the variety of forms and functions in which mentoring exists, and due to the range of contexts in which it takes place. Mentoring is fast becoming an everyday reality in education and other institutions. It is being increasingly used to support delivery of government policies on education, training and employment (National Mentoring Network, see www.nmn.org.uk for more information). Mentoring is frequently used in an attempt to engage underachieving individuals in the process of learning to develop their potential and therefore contribution to society as a whole (Gay and Richardson, 1998).

Mentoring disaffected talented pupils in PE

As seen in the previous chapter on recognising potential, talent development often involves recognising barriers to achievement and setting up support structures to allow potentially talented pupils the opportunities to overcome those barriers. Mentoring at this level can be achieved through the use of a learning mentor working with students within a school environment. The learning mentor could be:

- someone who has a dedicated role for behaviour improvement within the school, perhaps as part of a mentoring team
- a member of the pastoral team with a vested interest in working with someone in their particular year group or Key Stage
- a local coach, team manager or dance academy director
- someone from a local business
- a local professional sportsperson.

This follows the pattern of a mentoring relationship where an older, experienced person will work with a younger person, with the intention of helping to shape the growth and development of the mentee (Wright and Smith, 2000). Within the development of this relationship the identified aims of the learning mentor's role are to break down barriers to learning, unlock education opportunities for school students and release potential (DfES, 2001). However, in order for this to be established and implemented effectively, mentors must receive appropriate training and support and specific time must be allocated for the mentoring to occur. Potentially the individual pupils within a class who may benefit from this type of programme could be children who enjoy PE but are disaffected in other subject areas. The approach in this case may be to try to identify and transfer positive attributes gained in PE into other areas of the child's schooling. Alternatively, the child may be potentially gifted in terms of physical skill performance, but lack interpersonal skills which creates a barrier to them participating, particularly in team games. This disaffection may occur via lack of common beliefs and values or, as Ennis (1999) suggests, may be specific to PE where students find few meaningful connections between the curriculum and themselves. These scenarios present the question of how to integrate mentoring into PE so that target-setting strategies and systems to monitor and evaluate achievement can be utilised.

The focus on responsibility may be an appropriate starting point when supporting children who are disaffected from certain areas of their education, as responsibility is viewed by some as the foundation for allowing children to have a choice and a voice (Greenberg *et al.*, 1995). Developing a child's sense of personal and social responsibility will be vital to their success and fulfilment as it 'assumes an open future – one that we make ourselves, through our choices' (Stiehl, 1993: 71).

Consequently Hellison's (2003) aptly named 'responsibility model', which can be employed to encourage and promote educational values, offers a foundation upon which to structure the mentoring programme (Appendix 5.1) and individual education plan (IEP) (Appendix 5.2). The model's six levels suggest a focus upon self and social responsibility by empowering students to take more responsibility. The model then breaks down each goal, identifying methods of how this level may be achieved in practice.

Hellison's responsibility model

Level 0: Irresponsibility

- constantly make excuses
- blame others for their behaviour
- deny personal responsibility for what they do or fail to do.

Level 1: Self-control and respect for the rights and feelings of others

- lack of participation
- minimal signs of mastery or improvement
- don't interfere with other students' right to learn or teacher's right to teach
- don't require constant supervision to achieve this.

Level 2: Participation and effort

- at least minimal respect for others
- willingly play, accept challenges, practise skills
- under the teacher's supervision.

Level 3: Self-direction

- work without direct supervision
- identify own needs
- plan and carry out activities.

Level 4: Caring and helping

- respect others, self-directed
- cooperating with others
- give support, show concern and help others.

Level 5: Community, transfer of values to

- other subject areas – cross-curricular
- personal time – break, lunch, after-school clubs, own interest clubs
- home.

(from Hellison, 2003)

Through observation, negative aspects of the pupil's behaviour are noted on the individual education plan using the level criteria (see above) for guidance. For example, a pupil is observed as having 'minimal respect for others' within a lesson (Level 2).

Responsibility objectives are then designed in a positive manner and negotiated with the pupil. The use of 'working towards' and 'working beyond' within the objective will enable the negative aspect of the pupil's behaviour to be pitched in a positive manner. A starting point within the initial stages of the mentoring process could be to suggest that the pupil is working beyond Level 1 and a responsibility objective could be to show more respect for others by not deriding others' mistakes.

Self-evaluation through critical reflection is an intrinsic element of the process, particularly at the initial stages to increase the likelihood of ownership and the potential for empowerment. It is possible that pupils are at different levels within one lesson and it may be necessary to evaluate the pupil at their lowest level if an overall level grading is being used. Situations where 'cause and effect' can be cited will be useful to allow the pupil to see the result of their lack of responsibility. For example, if the cause of a pupil's lack of responsibility is that they 'blame others for their behaviour' the subsequent effect could be the negative experience the others are subject to as a result of being wrongly accused of something and the potential for the offending pupil to become ostracised from the group.

Considering the issues which have already been mentioned above, an IEP format sheet has been designed for potential use by learning mentors within physical education to integrate the theory via goals and strategies identified within the 'responsibility model' and place them into practice in conjunction with the underlying aims of the learning mentor's role. The flow chart in Appendix 5.1 summarises the processes involved in the mentoring process described above. This represents a tailored programme to suit an individual's needs. Mentoring would need to be established at an early stage to ensure the success of the IEP and also to create a flexible learning focus. Although the initial construction of the IEP can be time-consuming, due to pupils' unique needs, the flexibility of the strategy ensures that a diverse cohort of pupils may be accommodated.

Balancing sport, education and life

The level of support required for the talented pupil is highly dependent upon their ability to self-regulate. Whilst it is accepted that self-regulation is generally a characteristic associated with talented pupils, some pupils may require support in balancing their talents within physical education, and more specifically sport, with their educational and life demands elsewhere. The Junior Athlete Education (JAE) programme (see Youth Sport Trust, 2005, for more information) was established to meet the very needs of such pupils and school sport partnerships offer this level of support to some pupils who have demonstrated their potential by representing the county at one or more specific sports. While the downside to this particular level of support is the limited access to the scheme caused by the county level identification criteria; the support structure provided within this programme is commendable for the emphasis on maintaining strong levels of support in the school and home by involving a range of interested people. The JAE mentoring programme consists of the following components:

Young athlete workshop programme

- lifestyle management awareness
- performance profiling
- performance planning

Parents education workshop

- performance parents

Mentoring programme (low versus high need young athletes)

- group mentoring
- individual mentoring

The following diagram represents the philosophy behind such an approach.

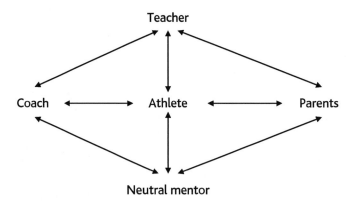

Junior Athlete Education programme – 'Team You'

Ofsted (2004) reported that mentoring, as a means of supporting talented pupils effectively, was present in the majority of schools it visited. Where schools had well established talent development programmes, ratios of talent support had been implemented to determine the level of assistance required. So pupils working at a national standard received adult to student ratios of 1:1 support whilst those at a school standard received 1:8. Of course the support required by pupils differs from one child to the next and there are variables over and above those of representative honours which will determine the level of support required. In some instances the pupil playing sport at national level may already have a supportive infrastructure provided through a particular national governing body which more than caters for their needs. Where the child does feel as if they are being supported effectively in this structure, the school may be better advised to turn their attention to those pupils demonstrating potential but unable to fulfil their potential for a variety of reasons (for more guidance on recognising potential refer to Chapter 3).

Mentoring high performance

The use of mentoring as a strategy for developing talented pupils in physical education is appropriate and timely when considering the influx of mentoring staff within schools. Mentoring is a specialist art and this factor may have led to a cautious approach to the area. However, now that fully trained professionals are on hand to offer support and indeed provide first-hand mentoring within their remit, the strategy of mentoring talented pupils has the potential to be a worthwhile venture. Similar approaches have been used in other talent development programmes (e.g. Youth Sport Trust, 2005).

Example of the strategy in practice

The Cooper's and Coborn Company School, Essex

Description

The school recognises the lifestyle demands associated with elite performance and has set up a mentoring strategy to support pupils who participate in competitive sport. The pupil–mentor ratio is dependant on performance levels with pupils performing at a national level receiving the most mentoring support (1:1). This provides the pupil with a consistent and reliable contact with whom they can meet regularly, discuss their progress at school, set realistic targets and develop support mechanisms to facilitate a balance between school work and sporting commitments. Mentors facilitate the pupils' school education across all areas of the curriculum.

Teachers' views

The head teacher at the school is very supportive and proud of the school's achievements in physical education and school sport. She became aware of certain out-of-school training commitments, and acted with the physical education department to set up an effective mentoring strategy to support their talented pupils:

'I suppose what brought it home to me was when I came to school one day and found my parking space was occupied by one of our students in the car with his father. It was 8 o'clock in the morning and he was having his breakfast. When I asked him "why?" I found out that he'd just completed two and a half hours swimming training at a local pool, and he was one of our most talented swimmers. My director of sport and I then discussed how we could actually balance work, life, study and training so that they didn't become disadvantaged in any of their academic work and they didn't become too tired.'

Flexible curriculum design

Flexible curriculum design is a strategy that offers support and recognises the commitments and lifestyle demands associated with elite performance. Like the 'mentoring high performance' strategy, the aims here are to support the individual needs of talented pupils and to minimise any conflict between the requirements of schoolwork and out-of-school participation in elite sport.

By adopting a pupil-centred approach, the school can create a flexible timetable designed specifically to suit the needs of the individual. Raising staff awareness of any issues involved such as nutritional requirements can also assist the pupil in achieving their goals.

Example of the strategy in practice

The Deanes School, Essex

Description

The Deanes School appreciates the lifestyle demands associated with high level performance. In this example, two elite tennis players in Year 8 and their coach explain how the school has created a flexible timetable to facilitate their tennis development. The coach works with both the pupils using the sports college facilities during curriculum time to ensure that they receive the quality of provision required.

Coach's views

'The flexible timetable was used because we felt that if we could identify areas where the students would benefit from a tennis lesson perhaps instead of being in their normal mainstream lesson ... it may take some of the pressure off and it would mean that they could get some extra tennis training and physical training as part of their normal day as opposed to being up very late at night, training at clubs ... it eased the time pressures.'

Pupils' views

Initially, the pupils were concerned with missing the same lessons which could cause problems in certain subject areas. This concern was addressed by creating different timetables for each week to avoid the pupils missing the same lessons consecutively. The pupils felt that this method helped their tennis development and minimised conflict with their school work:

'Last year, we had one timetable, so you'd miss every lesson. But now we've got two timetables, you miss like a different lesson each week, that's what I like about it.'

CHAPTER 6

Beyond the curriculum

In the twenty-first century, physical education and school sport do not sit in isolation. As part of the world of grass roots sport, provision for all students can be developed and delivered with the assistance of professionals and volunteers from a range of organisations. The knowledge and perspectives possessed by these individuals can be of great value in producing holistic, child-centred programmes for gifted and talented students.

School to club

It is not enough that a high quality development pathway from school to club and beyond is in place. If their talented pupils are going to benefit, schools must in the first place actually be aware of its existence and secondly know-how to access it. In the first instance it is up to those working at the strategic level within school sport partnerships to forge an understanding as to what the pathway is all about, with their counterparts in national governing bodies and county sports partnerships. However the whole process becomes impotent if knowledge remains at this level only. For the widest number of gifted and talented pupils to benefit from the talent development pathways that are being developed and updated by NGBs and their partners, school sport partnerships must disseminate knowledge downwards. School sport coordinators, heads of PE, PE departments, primary link teachers, even peripatetic coaches or non-specialist teachers taking extracurricular activities must be involved. Whilst it might be unrealistic to expect all of these individuals to have comprehensive knowledge of the mechanics of all talent development pathways, they all need to be aware of the pathways' existence and how to access them.

The notion of club-school partnership must be more than a glorified talent spotting exercise, organised by a teacher or parent who had a stake in a particular club or interest in a certain sport. The odd poster here and there, or worse still leaving things to word of mouth, is unlikely to produce intended outcomes.

County sports partnerships and the local development officers of national sports governing bodies are now working with a selection of focus clubs, considered to have what it takes in terms of facilities, ethos and expertise, to provide a high-quality experience. It will also be possible to obtain contacts for clubs whose sport is not a focus area for local sports development. For these, the Sport England website (www.sportengland.org/index/a-z_index.htm) is a good place to start. As well as being a forum through which to develop talented youngsters, club-school partnerships now must have a much broader *raison d'être*. With inclusion high on both the educational and sporting agendas, partnerships developed by clubs and schools must target all children. With pressure to widen participation levels in both school and community sport growing, schools must also look to work with a broad range of sports. Of course, talented youngsters must be given a chance to shine, but when developing these partnerships, schools also need to find out how a variety of clubs can engage the widest possible number of their youngsters and sustain their involvement.

In order to be successful club-school partnerships must be organised much more thoroughly than was once the case. There is so much going on today that children can do instead of sport, so unless programmes are designed well, youngsters will simply not get involved. Planning is crucial here and will usually involve the creation of some sort of schedule of events – perhaps involving taster sessions and after-school clubs at the school, some form of competition and finally some activity at the club itself.

Although there is no one right way of organising a club-school partnership, the following general advice can be given:

- come to an agreement about the aims of the partnership and what both school and club need to do in order to ensure its success

- design programmes collaboratively – deciding which children to target, why, when and how

- ensure these schemes do not stand alone but instead contribute to, or at very least complement, the core purpose of each partner organisation

- take ownership of the whole scheme, not just the parts which directly benefit the school

- proactively market all elements of the programme to ensure maximum attendance

- think about how and when to manage the transition process from school to club activity, so as to reduce the dropout rate, often associated with changing times and venues of activity

- involve the local official sporting infrastructure who will be able to suggest their own ways of developing, supporting and sustaining the partnership

- get feedback from participants as to positive and negative aspects of the scheme and act on these to increase levels of involvement

● look at other such projects that have worked well and try and isolate the reasons for their success. Try and apply them to what you yourselves are trying to achieve.

According to Graham Ross – Sport England's senior development manager for talent – schools need to contribute to a collaborative approach to developing sporting talent. Commenting on what in particular the school–club relationship should look like in the future, he said: 'The gifted and talented strand of the PESSCL programme focuses on defining quality standards and supporting children through Junior Athlete Education (JAE) and mentoring at a time when often sporting and academic pressures coincide.

'The challenge now and for the future is to ensure that young people are offered "high quality" and complementary sporting opportunities in the community, to find and work with clubs that can cater for those with ambition and talent and assist them in following a performance pathway.'

To this end, many national governing bodies of sport are developing, promoting and implementing their own talent frameworks. Often referred to as long-term athlete/player development frameworks, they outline in general terms what type of coaching competition and rest/recovery programmes should be followed at each age/stage from early experience through to high performance levels, to enable individuals to maximise their sporting talent.

A key aspect to this is an understanding of the needs of early and late developers in terms of identifying, developing and supporting talented individuals. National governing bodies are in the process of updating their coach education programmes to assist coaches in becoming more equipped to deliver at each stage of the player pathway. Gradually, this knowledge should filter down into clubs and by accessing sports development networks through the local school sport partnership, it will be possible to identify those clubs with the necessary expertise to develop the talented individual.

It does have to be remembered however that we are dealing with human beings and not robots that can be programmed to operate in a certain desired direction. Although teachers and coaches may be of the opinion that a talented youngster would be better served at a certain club, that does not mean the youngster themselves – who may already be having a great time with friends at another – will agree. Indeed, pressurising a player to uproot and move to unfamiliar surroundings could undermine that youngster's determination to continue playing altogether. Encouraging one of their top young players to join another club could also threaten the school's relationship with the first club. This club may actually be providing a good quality inclusive experience for many students from the school, even if it lacks the expertise and perspective to fully develop the really talented player.

Key to the successful management of this whole process is awareness. Is the player fully aware of their own potential and what needs to be done to reach it? Are they happy being a big fish in a small pond or do they really want to push themselves to be the best they can? Are teachers aware of the youngster's level of desire and commitment and of his or her potential to cope in unfamiliar surroundings? Is the club in question aware of the limitations of its own expertise and of its essential role in the development of a player? Lastly, are parents aware of what it will be necessary for them to do to support their child should he or she decide to move further afield to a club more suited to developing talented performers? Are they in a position to do so?

Open discussions involving all parties should be able to come to a sensible solution based on what is best for the youngster in question.

The national competition framework for schools

Competition is one of the most powerful tools available to a PE department. If pitched correctly and if the needs of the children and not of whatever team they happen to be playing for are put first, competition can enthuse and encourage involvement. It can also give youngsters a reason to want to develop their skills.

Taking a laissez-faire, or worse still an outcome orientated 'win at all costs' approach, is likely to result in a whole host of inequalities. Whilst talented players cruise through easy matches, their skill levels hardly taxed let alone improved by the experience; less able students or, worse still, beginners with potential but little experience will be unable to cope and might even be put off from playing sport altogether.

Subject to consultation, the national competition framework for schools will look like the table opposite.

So for all children, competitive situations must be an experience they can enjoy and learn from. They must take into account both where the children are in terms of development and also where they are looking to go. It must stretch them but at the same time provide realistic goals, which it is within the students' power to achieve. Of course there will always be winners and losers but competitive situations must be generated where a one-sided outcome is not a foregone conclusion, however well or badly each set of youngsters perform in relation to their own ability.

The emerging Schools Competition Framework aims to design appropriate programmes for young people of all ages and abilities. While it is hard to generalise, many sports at present have duplicate structures which often mean that tensions exist between school and club commitments. The competition framework will offer the opportunity for sports to develop and implement new school competitive programmes that can then effectively link and integrate with the competitive opportunities on the NGB pathway.

However this new framework will not transform things overnight – neither is it meant to be a quick fix solution. There are many entrenched attitudes in schools and clubs that need to be challenged. Even parents – who might encourage their child to play a particular position in a particular sport over and over again, at the expense of that child's all-round sporting experience – need to be educated.

The national competition framework

Stage	Competition
Key Stage 1 5–7 years	• annual off-site multi-skill (fun) festival • working across clusters (beyond peer group) • secondary schools organise for primaries • possible multi-sport award schemes and log books for young people
Key Stage 2 7–9 years	• multi-skill festivals (termly) • off school site • 'theme' based • possible early specialisation in some sports through NGB and club structure
Key Stage 2 9–11 years	• multi-sport competition (6 week block rotation) • central venue leagues • coaching and competition based on primary, secondary or club sites
Key Stage 3 11–12 years	• multi-sport competition (monthly 3 sports) • e.g. central venue leagues in a range of sports coaching and competition at secondary, hub or club sites
Key Stage 3 & 4 12–16 years	• interschool leagues and cup competitions within school sport partnerships (year group teams) • identification of national 'core' sports plus additional sports identified locally (NGBs would have to have an integrated competitive structure including schools associations accepted as core)
16–19 years	• not for talented students already identified as part of NGB talent programmes • 'junior varsity' to give this group an identity • intramural competition within the learning community – schools/PE/6th forms • organised sport in core sports that match the secondary programmes. • e.g. single-venue festivals for a number of institutions during ring-fenced time (Wednesday pm)

For more information visit www.culture.gov.uk/sport/school_sport/competition_managers.htm

Taking a collaborative approach will be key to implementing the competition framework on the ground. Aligning and integrating school PE and sporting opportunities in the community will help to ensure the young person has a clearer and smoother journey through the sports system that enables them to make the best of their sporting abilities.

A programme that has a realistic understanding of the young person's needs and wishes, rather than the interests of school, club or parents, as its central focus, is what is needed. Schools should be working towards this, not just for their gifted and talented students, but for all their young people.

The National Academy for Gifted and Talented Youth

www.nagty.ac.uk

The National Academy for Gifted and Talented Youth (NAGTY) was established by the UK government in 2002 to drive forward work in gifted and talented education across the country. NAGTY develops, promotes and supports the provision of educational opportunities for gifted and talented children and young people aged up to 19. It aims to supply academic and professional expertise to national policymakers and school practitioners, and acts as a catalyst for developing understanding in the teaching profession.

NAGTY's mission is:

- to dedicate its energies, skills and expertise to ensure that gifted and talented children in England are given the opportunity and support to maximise their potential

- to ensure that teachers and members of the education profession have the knowledge, skills and support to meet the needs of gifted and talented children

- to develop and enhance its unique national role to become the leading world centre of integrated research, innovation and practical implementation in the field of gifted and talented education.

Its principal supporting aims are:

- to identify gifted and talented pupils throughout England and to ensure provision of a range of in and out-of-school opportunities, guidance and support which will boost their attainment, aspiration, motivation and self-confidence

- to apply its expertise to national policy issues and contribute significantly to the government's strategy for gifted and talented children

- to extend and deepen the knowledge and professional skills of all involved in the planning and delivery of gifted and talented education.

Working with a range of national and regional partners through its professional and student academies, NAGTY leads an approach to gifted and talented education for the top 5 per cent of the population which blends high quality in-school learning with additional learning opportunities, offered face-to-face and electronically. NAGTY calls this the 'English model' of gifted and talented education (Campbell *et al.*, 2004), and it is becoming increasingly visible in schools across the UK and has attracted a significant amount of interest from overseas. This approach is also a key component of delivering the government's personalised learning agenda for gifted and talented young people.

At the time of writing, NAGTY has over 46,000 members enrolled from all areas of England. One area of activity within the student academy that has attracted much interest has been the NAGTY summer school programme. Summer schools are residential courses of two or three weeks in length for students aged 11–16. The courses are run at universities across England and students are taught by a teaching team including academics, teachers and current postgraduate students.

NAGTY programmes

The idea of a residential summer school for the most gifted pupils from across the country is based on a model that has been in existence for some years in the United States, especially the well-established Johns Hopkins Centre for Talented Youth (CTY) model. However, over time the CTY and NAGTY models have become markedly different. For example, unlike their US colleagues, NAGTY summer schools take place at a number of leading universities, at different locations across England, with staff there coordinating the planning and running of courses and hiring of staff. This enables the course deliverers to develop courses matched to their expertise and the needs of the students over time.

In 2005, NAGTY summer schools were offered by the following institutions:

- Canterbury Christ Church University (South East)

- University of Durham (North East)

- University of Exeter (South West)

- Imperial College (London)

- Lancaster University (North West)

- University of Warwick (Midlands)

- University of York (North East).

The courses offered vary by institution, but a typical programme would include mathematics, English, a science and modern foreign languages. Pupils choose to follow one course for the duration of the school, and join the pupils attending different courses at their university for social and sporting activities for evenings and at weekends. Pupils attended summer schools from all areas of England and, interestingly, most of them preferred not to attend the university nearest to their home.

Alongside summer school programmes, NAGTY also coordinates a national programme of 'outreach' events. These are short courses that normally take place at weekends or during school holidays. They are delivered by experts in their field and cover a wide range of academic subject areas. Programmes take place all over England and the number of locations is growing constantly. In theory, outreach events could be residential. However, in practice, the great majority are not, and consequently primarily attract pupils from relatively local areas.

Considering the focus of this book, it is important to note that, to date, NAGTY has not focused, at all, on the so-called 'talent' subjects. Its provision has been directed very much at 'gifted' learners. Pupils who are talented in physical education, therefore, have not significantly benefited from such experiences. Of course, the peculiar classification of gifted and talented education means that there is no necessary reason to exclude those with an exceptional ability in physical education, so long as that ability is an academic one. So, for example, at least one summer school course on offer in recent years has been 'sport science', which emphasised the theoretical and scientific aspects of physical and sporting performance. Despite the current limitations of NAGTY's provision in the area of physical education, it is important for teachers to know about its work for two reasons:

1. NAGTY is still a relatively new organisation, and there is a great likelihood that its narrow focus on the gifted subjects will broaden out to include the full scope of curriculum areas, including physical education.

2. Academically gifted pupils in physical education have educational needs too, and these are currently overlooked by practice-based provision; so NAGTY-type courses are likely to remain the most appropriate opportunities for them.

Multi-skilling talented pupils in physical education and sport

Introduction

There has been a recent proliferation of multi-skill opportunities in England, predominantly for children of primary school age. However, as a tool for talent development, use of the term 'multi-skills' is relatively novel and seemingly embraces the use of movement skills in a non-sports specific manner. In this country at least, multi-skills, as a generic concept, seems to have evolved from the need to harness the development of fundamental movement skills (FMS) or 'observable, goal-directed movement patterns' (Burton and Miller, 1998: 5.) inherent in developing youngsters.

At its core this relates to the development of movement skills such as balance, coordination, reaction and timing. These FMS are the essence of sport and physical activity and are often seen as contributory to the overall player pathway of the athlete as they progress through their recognised developmental stages.

A number of national governing bodies have recently adopted the Long-Term Athlete Development (LTAD) programme, which suggests that up until the age of 12 for late specialisation sports the athlete should not be primarily concerned with acquiring sport-specific skills and instead should concentrate on a range of 'FUNdamentals' and 'learning to train' which align closely to the components within a multi-skill programme. In accordance with this principle, the Department for Culture, Media and Sport (DCMS) and the Department for Education and Skills (DfES) have both endorsed a multi-skills approach, with a variety of motives, under the auspices of the Physical Education, School Sport and Club Links strategy (PESSCL) through the establishment of multi-skill clubs (MS clubs) and multi-skill academies (MSA) respectively.

The inclusion of multi-skills within PESSCL is becoming more noticeable as new initiatives and employment opportunities emerge. For example, the schools competition framework will ensure the linkage between competitions and the multi-skills framework as part of the competition manager's remit (Teachernet, 2005). Moreover, local sports delivery units are actively advertising for personnel to be employed with explicit remits to deliver multi-skill activities. The creation of multi-skill clubs is viewed as contributing towards the DCMS (DCMS, 2005a) delivery targets that 'by 2008, 85 per cent of 5–16 year olds are getting two hours a week of high quality PE and sport' (p. 26) and 'every child will have two hours of school sport by 2010, with another two to three hours outside of school' (p. 26).

Talent development pathways are also considered within the rationale for the establishment of multi-skills in that they are included in a generic sense in the 'building foundations for elite sport' plans (DCMS, 2005a, p. 32). There is a clear link also between LTAD and multi-skills in the method of approach that sports agencies are adopting in the guidelines given for the holistic development of the talented athlete (Sportscoach UK, 2005).

The use of fundamental movement skills in a multi-skills environment

Multi-skills objectives and content (Youth Sport Trust, 2004; Sherwood, 2005) relate closely to theoretical principles relating to the development of a child's FMS (Burton and Miller, 1998; Vereijken and Bongaardt, 1999). Indeed, there is a direct correlation between guidance for the use of specific multi-skill activities and the use of activities used to assess FMS in relation to physical activity (Youth Sport Trust, 2004; Okely *et al.*, 2001). Although research involving the use of a multi-skills environment is limited there is empirical and conceptual literature that relates to the development and assessment of FMS. Indeed, the range and amount of literature relating to FMS, motor skill acquisition and related fields is immense. Therefore, for the purpose of this chapter, areas of relevance to the current context of multi-skill development within the existing multi-skill framework will be prioritised.

As with many teaching practices the use of assessment to inform teaching and learning is instrumental in the pedagogical understanding of the acquisition of new skills. Hands (2002) discusses the qualitative and quantitative nature of assessing FMS, and assessment is viewed as being fit for purpose, with some of those purposes most salient to this context being to provide feedback to the performer or to predict performance in the future (Burton and Miller, 1998). Quantitative measures of movement skill proficiency through the employment of screening tests allow for the testing of large groups with minimal understanding of the tester in terms of movement competencies. Tests of this nature are currently used in schools as part of a school's PE talent development programme (Bailey, Morley and Dismore, 2005) and have been documented in a case study format (Tremere, Morley and Bailey, 2005). Although these forms of tests minimise standardisation problems between testers and ensure a high level of reliability in terms of tracking and profiling, the quality of the movement is not assessed. Moreover, factors inherent in a high level or low level performance are not observed and the development of future programmes may not be influenced by this feedback.

Qualitative assessment, looking at how the skill is performed, seems to have taken centre stage recently with the use of observation sheets and criteria checklists designed to inform the most appropriate subsequent intervention to enhance performance. Once assessment of a qualitative nature has been conducted there is more opportunity to facilitate the child's progression through the developmental stages of motor learning as proposed by various theorists (Gallahue, 1982; Jess and Collins, 2003). An example of the qualitative nature of assessment that has recently been developed in the UK is the CD resource 'Observing Children Moving' (Maude and Whitehead, 2003) that seeks to support teachers in the identification of movement through a series of movement capabilities and associated tasks.

In the dynamic systems model of skill acquisition, an emphasis is made upon the 'importance of exploration' and the requirement for children not to repeat through repetition but by refining movements for a better outcome (Vereijken and Bongaardt, 1999). This approach has resonance with the multi-skill guidelines that recommend multi-skills sessions utilise a range of activities and exercises which are not always directly relevant to a particular movement within a recognised sport. There is also credibility in the motive of the recently established multi-skills environments, in their efforts to lead children on to further development of FMS by suggesting links to other clubs, as it has been suggested that improved performance of FMS has a positive relationship with participation in organised sport (Okely *et al.*, 2001).

Gender differences in mastery of FMS have been well documented (Walkley *et al.*, 1993; Raudsepp and Paasuke, 1995) with one study showing that in particular skills (balance) there was no gender difference in acquisition and others (throw and kick) were mastered the best by boys and the poorest by girls. Conversely, the hop and side gallop was mastered the best by girls and was among the more poorly performed skills for the boys (Van Buerden *et al.*, 2002). Gender differences are an integral part of one strand of Singer's (1982) interpretation of the main considerations in understanding how people learn skills and these can be categorised as follows:

1. learning and performance processes (processes that seem to work the same for most people)

2. individual differences (ways in which people seem to differ in terms of how they learn and respond to situations)

3. instructional conditions (ways in which to manipulate learning environments or tasks in order to facilitate learning for people in general with respect to individual differences).

Multi-skill clubs

Multi-skill clubs (MS clubs) were launched in February 2005 (Youth Sport Trust, 2005) and form the foundation of the multi-skills pathway through the facilitation of wide scale access onto an activity programme. The clubs are for children between Years 3 and 6 (7–11 year olds) and involve the delivery of units of work, with a central focus on ABCs (agility, balance and coordination), normally outside of school hours, by a community coach or qualified teacher. There is a strong emphasis on links between the school sport partnership (SSP) and the county sports partnership in the design and delivery of multi-skill clubs. The clubs are funded by DCMS and it is expected that there will be approximately 650 clubs by September 2006 (DCMS, 2005b).

MS clubs may provide the first club experience for a young person and as such are intended to bridge the school to community gap and create the first step from school sport to club sport and there is evidence of SSPs already establishing MS clubs in some areas of the country (West Yorkshire Sport, 2005).

As well as the attention to the actual performance of the movement skills, the resource cards for the clubs will also ask practitioners to consider the cognitive processes involved in performing the various movements through a delivery strategy involving use of the mnemonic FABB (feet, arms, body and brain). There is anecdotal evidence to suggest multi-skill clubs may contribute towards a rise in self-esteem and increased motivation in aspects of schooling other than PE (QCA, 2005). Resourcing and funding for MS clubs is based on a phased approach using the different establishment levels of SSPs to direct the process. For more information visit www.talentladder.org.uk

Multi-skill academies

Multi-skill academies (MSAs) are funded through the DfES, again under the auspices of the PESSCL strategy, and aim to develop talented pupils in PE and sport through the creation of a programme of activities which are delivered normally during a school holiday or as an after-school activity. MSAs are hosted by a specialist sports college within a SSP and delivered by PE teachers and/or coaches where appropriate.

The academies are designed to offer a range of activities that develop pupils' ability to perform and understand fundamental movement skills, develop game playing abilities, and also 'identify potentially talented young people for national governing body (LTAD) programmes' (Smith, 2005). Selection for attendance is conducted within primary schools attached to the SSP and exemplified within an information and guidance pack (Youth Sport Trust, 2004) which offers an identification template similar to the National Curriculum level descriptors for Key Stage 2 (DfEE, 1999b).

The growth of MS academies over the past two years combined with the case study approach to guiding the programme within them has led to a widespread interpretation of what actually constitutes a MSA environment and the range of activities and principles used within MSA programmes prove this. What seems to be the consensus across all case study examples of programme content is the lack of sport-specific type of practice with the academies and the stipulation that fundamental generalised movement skills form the core of activities. What is not so apparent is the influence of National Curriculum objectives on the design of multi-skill programmes and the linkage between the experiences within curricular physical education and the academies. As selection is conducted at primary school level, with the primary link teachers and school sport coordinator more often than not working in partnership to identify the talented pupils, it is not always clear to see what the identification process should entail.

Coupled with the initial identification process is also the issue of standardisation and moderation across the SSP and the measures taken to promote a consensus of agreement. Agreement, in terms of the synergy between curricular PE and the multi-skill pathway, is another area of potential ambiguity. Other studies of talent development have suggested a great deal of uncertainty in the identification of talent in PE, with talent in sport often dominating the process (Morley, Bailey and Holt, 2003; Bailey *et al.* 2004). There is a legitimate concern that such a course of action could be replicated within the identification of talent for selection onto a multi-skill academy. The following diagram represents the intended place of multi-skills in the performance pathways of young people.

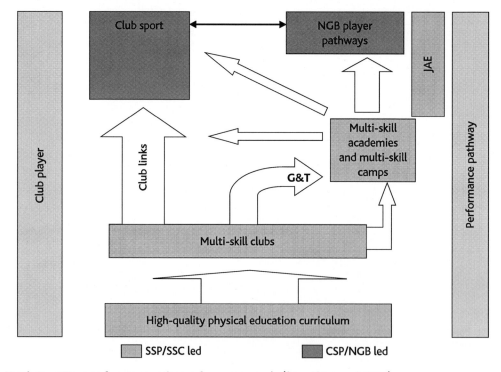

Youth Sport Trust performance pathways for young people (from Sherwood, 2005)

Multi-skill camps

The multi-skill camp (MS camp) is not a part of the current formalised hierarchy of multi-skills development. This section will detail the design of a regional MS camp specifically conceived to pilot the potential for an additional phase of multi-skill development beyond the experiences of the MS clubs and MSAs. The following diagram summarises the existing multi-skill framework and introduces the concept of the MS camp as the third tier of that provision.

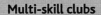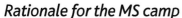

Multi-skill camps
End of Year 6 pupils (Aged 11/12)
Regionally based children selected from primary schools
based on physical, creative, cognitive, personal and social ability
Delivered by PE staff/coaches

Multi-skill academies
150 in 2005
Typically 40–80 Year 6/7 pupils (aged 11–13)
Based at SSC – children selected from primary schools,
MS clubs, PE lessons and clubs
Delivered by PE staff/coaches

Multi-skill clubs
650 by Sep 2006
Year 3–6 pupils (Aged 7–11)
Based at sports centres/schools – open access,
resource cards provided – ABCs & FABB
Delivered by community sport coaches, PE staff

A proposed **three-tier approach to multi-skills provision**

Rationale for the MS camp

The MS camp was established in order to extend and enrich the experiences gained by children participating at the higher end of the multi-skill spectrum in a multi-skill, multi-activity and multi-ability environment. The camp also sought to establish identification criteria that would engage a wide range of talented children from a number of talent domains in PE and to subsequently design, deliver and evaluate a programme of activities that was stimulating, challenging, innovative and relevant for talented children in physical education and sport. The recent introduction of a model and guidance for talent development in physical education (Bailey and Morley, 2003), a multi-skills environment (Smith, 2005; Sherwood, 2005) and sport (Balyi and Hamilton, 2000) meant that the MS camp aims and objectives needed to be cognisant of a range of emerging talent pathways.

Identification and selection

Partnership development managers (PDM) from all 27 school sport partnerships (SSPs) within Yorkshire were invited to a launch where the process of identification was discussed as well as the draft programme outline and research activities. The process of identification was guided by an identification template (shown overleaf) that was designed by superimposing the five abilities suggested by Bailey and Morley's model for talent development in PE (provided in full in

Multi-skill camp identification template	Rating
Complete this for pupils who demonstrate **talent in PE** Please respond: 5=Excellent 4=Very good 3=Good 2=Satisfactory 1=Requires support	
Pupil's name: **School:**	
Physical	
Explores and develops skills demonstrating control, fluency and quality in a range of activities	
Demonstrates a range of skills in different compositional and tactical situations	
Demonstrates good peripheral vision and uses this in a range of situations across activities	
Shows precision when executing movement skills with high levels of coordination and balance	
Sub-total	
Social	
Demonstrates the ability to take the lead when working with others	
Communicates clearly to others when describing their performances showing an understanding of tactics/strategies and compositional ideas	
Demonstrates the ability to make good decisions when working collaboratively	
Enables and empowers other pupils in participating effectively in activities	
Sub-total	

Personal	
Shows motivation, commitment and focus when working	
Demonstrates the ability to self-regulate learning in independent learning environments	
Demonstrates the ability to evaluate their own performance effectively	
Handles feedback in a constructive way and uses this to develop levels of performance	
Sub-total	
Cognitive	
Demonstrates the ability to transfer skills effectively across a range of activities	
Demonstrates the ability to plan and utilise a range of strategies in a number of activities	
Identifies strengths and weaknesses, offering suggestions for improvement, across a range of performances	
Uses a broad analysis vocabulary when describing performances	
Sub-total	
Creative	
Consolidates and develops skills in a creative, inventive and innovative way	
Responds to stimulus in an innovative way	
Offers a range of productive and viable solutions to a problem	
Is confident in experimenting with acquired skills and ideas through application (e.g. within a gymnastic sequence, dance composition or game)	
Total	

Chapter 5) into end of Key Stage 2 level descriptors from the National Curriculum for PE, while maintaining comparability to the existing MSA framework for identification. This meant, in theory, that pupils would be identified and selected by being given ratings for their talents within four distinct domains:

- cognitive ability

- physical ability

- social ability

- creative ability.

The fifth disposition of talent according to Bailey and Morley's model, that of personal ability, was used as a deciding factor should the ratings of pupils in a SSP be equal at the end of the identification process. The decision to identify the participants in this particular way was driven by the emergence of a model for talent development in PE and the perceived requirement of the camp to identify a broad range of talent within physical education. It was felt more appropriate to use a PE environment as the primary source of identification as this domain is more inclusive (i.e. every child will normally access it), and PDMs and SSCos generally have more input into this area in comparison to their work with community clubs or national governing body representatives.

Groupings

Once selected, pupils were grouped by the four abilities for their time on the camp, e.g. 20 pupils were invited to attend the MS camp as a result of their high levels of creativity in PE. Other options were considered for the grouping of participants for the camp; these ranged from random grouping to grouping by sporting interests or geographical location. However, grouping by specific ability was deemed the most appropriate in order to provide a range of tailored activities to meet the participants' needs.

Activities

Eight activities were delivered across two days to all groups. The selection of the range of activities for use on the MS camp was determined by the alliance of the activity to the following key requirements:

- related to NCPE areas of activity

- novelty – unlikely to have experienced specific activities before in Key Stages 1 and 2 PE

- facilitates environment for children with a range of abilities

- non-sports specific.

With these requirements in mind the following activities were selected for use on the camp:

- athletic challenges

- speed, agility and quickness

- core stability and balance using gymnastic activities

- games for development 1 (Tchoukball, see www.tchoukball.org.uk for more information)

- games for development 2 (square ball, a game invented for specific use on the camp)

- body management through dance activities (based on the dance production 'stomp', visit www.stomponline.com for more information)

- team building through physical challenges

- problem solving using aquatic activities (water polo)

- understanding nutrition for performance and health.

As the participants were grouped by specific ability each activity had a number of core tasks but was modified to suit the needs of the group as they rotated through the activity programme. For example, when the 'physical' group participated in the dance activity, an emphasis was placed on the acquisition of body movements to form a motif and subsequent expression through actual movement, whereas the 'creative' group investigated ways of communicating with each other and experimenting with a variety of approaches to solve the task – the end product was not deemed to be as critical.

Although the camp was deemed a huge success by all parties involved, the potential for its development, at the time of writing, remains unclear. However, the following recommendations may prove useful in assisting those practitioners responsible for organising MS clubs and MSAs.

Recommendations

- MS providers must inform the intended participants of the nature and aims of the camp more effectively in order to alleviate any misconceptions in expectations.

- Evaluations must be conducted to investigate the aims, content and delivery and participants' perceptions of MS clubs and MSAs to accurately assess the development of a child within the whole multi-skill framework.

- A developmental approach to identification and selection, and design of activities and grouping, must be considered throughout the multi-skills framework to ensure a coherent talent development pathway for the children involved within it.

- A rigorous standardisation process must precede the talent identification phase of any selective MS provision.

- Subsequent provision for MS participants in the PE curriculum, extracurricular and out-of-school activities needs to be considered in respect of experiences and benefits gained from attendance at the camp.

Higher education institutions

Higher education institutions (HEIs) are able to provide an additional level of support for schools in their efforts to meet the needs of their gifted and talented students. In general, HEIs can offer a range of specialist expertise and facilities as well as an inspiring location for students to work in. For their part, universities will wish to target gifted youngsters as these students are their most likely future applicants. With so many sports related courses available these days, HEIs can be a valuable partner, assisting schools in maintaining a student's involvement in physical education and sustaining a talented performer's involvement in sport.

Not only can on-site activities extend and enrich the curricular experiences of gifted and talented pupils, but working alongside HEI experts can assist the development of innovative new provision strategies that can be used in school.

Leeds Metropolitan University

One such recent collaboration has been between Leeds Metropolitan University and a nearby school. Held at the university, the day included an introduction and tour of the campus facilities plus the following four sessions.

Sports nutrition

A general introduction to macro-nutrients and the energy requirements of athletes followed by a specific focus on sports drinks. This provides enrichment and extension to the following areas of the AQA 2006 A/AS Sport and PE syllabus (p. 34):

- energy sources
- effects of intensity on energy sources (respiratory quotient)
- glycogen depletion/loading.

Exercise physiology

Laboratory testing demonstration including a progressive intensity protocol (treadmill) to measure levels of blood lactate, maximal oxygen uptake (VO2 max), respiratory quotient (RQ) and fluid loss. This provides enrichment and extension to the following areas of the AQA syllabus (pp. 33–34):

- energy systems
- oxygen deficit

- VO2 max
- OBLA.

Principles of training

A practical session to demonstrate heart rate response and the benefits of various training principles. This provides enrichment and extension to the following areas of the AQA syllabus (pp. 30–31):

- heart rate zones
- planning, performing and evaluating exercise programmes
- principles of training.

Lifestyle management

An opportunity to look at strategies to balance lifestyle demands to achieve success in sport, education and work. Not directly related to the AQA syllabus but considered to be useful in terms of the students' personal needs and career aspirations.

Although targeted specifically at A/AS level students, there is no reason why a similar arrangement could not be made for pupils taking GCSE PE. Of course the focus of activities would have to be changed to fit in with course requirements, but the following advice from Richard Tremere of Leeds Metropolitan University on how to go about organising such an event would remain the same.

- Think about which students to select. The more the better, but make sure that each youngster has been targeted for a specific reason.

- Be clear about why you are setting the event up – have clear objectives for the day and plan out exactly how the experience will enrich the studies of the students involved.

- Prior to the event, determine a series of intended outcomes against which success can be measured at a later date.

- Build into the event ways of engaging students into the world of higher education.

Conclusion – a model of talent development in PE

In order to draw together all of the concepts, practices, ideas and principles presented in this book, this final section presents a model of talent development in physical education. To the best of our knowledge, no such model has been published before. However, in light of the UK government's expectation that all curriculum subjects identify and provide for a cohort of very able, or in the language of the day, 'gifted and talented' students, this is a timely task.

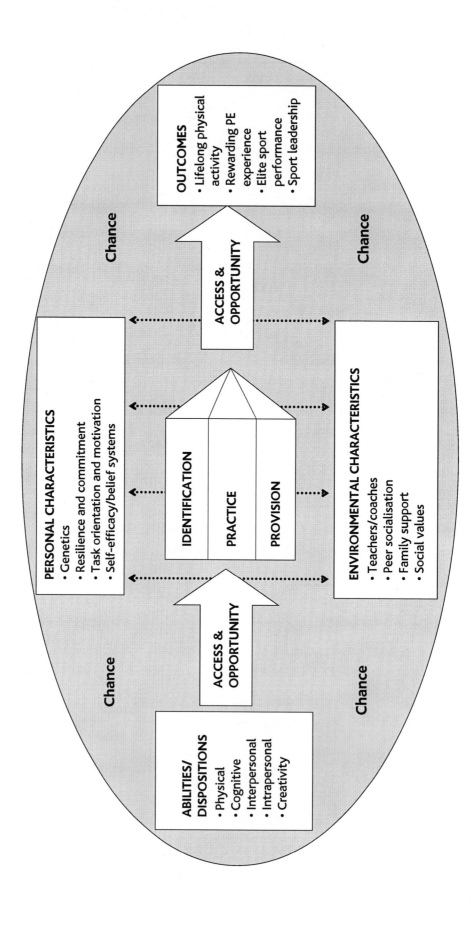

A model of talent development in physical education

In presenting a model, we aim to make explicit our theorising about the nature, content and character of the talent development process in physical education. We prefer the term 'model' to describe our presentation to the more ambitious 'theory' as the process of talent development in physical education is very much in its infancy. Indeed, academic discussions of talent within the context of curricular physical education are almost non-existent (exceptions include Bailey and Morley, 2003; Kirk and Gorely, 2000; Penney, 2000; Macfadyen and Bailey, 2002). In designing the model, we have drawn on a variety of sources and exemplars, particularly from sport and education (such as Abbott *et al.*, 2002; Regnier *et al.*, 1993; Heller *et al.*, 2000), and have generally found multi-dimensional, developmental educational models (Gagné, 2000; Perleth and Heller, 1994; Schoon, 2000) most suitable, for reasons that should become clear in the text.

Our model describes a framework for investigating the actualisation of abilities related to physical education, and, in doing so, it draws together a wide range of evidence, analogy and theory, framed within value judgements regarding the nature and purpose of physical education.

Appendices

Ofsted – Expectations of schools in relation to able pupils

Evaluation focus	Issue	Judgement/evidence
Effectiveness of school	Inclusion/equal opportunities	● High achievement is determined by 'the school's commitment to inclusion and the steps it takes to ensure that *every* pupil does as well as possible.' (p. 25) ● At the parents' meeting, inspectors should find out if, in the view of parents, 'their children are progressing as well as they could; their children are happy in school, well taught and well cared for; the extent to which the school promotes equality of opportunity between different groups and includes *all* pupils and parents.' (p. 38)
Standards achieved by pupils	Achievement and underachievement	● Inspectors are asked to look at the achievement of different groups. (p. 44) ● 'If they (pupils) are readily capable of work beyond that which they are doing, they are underachieving.' (p. 45) ● A school should know 'how well gifted and talented pupils do and, where appropriate, how well pupils do in the school's specialist subjects . . . Inspectors should judge how well the school uses information to identify and deal with underachievement, challenge the most capable and raise standards for all pupils.' (p. 48)
	Early entry	● Inspectors should be aware of special circumstances, such as 'a school policy on early entry for GCSE for some pupils.' ● 'Where pupils are entered early for GCSE examinations, inspectors should take account of the results in reaching a judgement about the performance of the year group as a whole and consider what early entry has allowed the pupils to achieve subsequently.' (p. 47)
	Discussion with pupils	● Inspectors should 'talk to pupils of different ages and levels of attainment (including) . . . the high achievers.' (p. 54)
	Assessment	● Assessment might guide planning through 'review of pupils' progress, including whether targets have been met at the end of a unit of work to inform teaching and target-setting for the whole class, groups and individuals.' (p. 88) ● Inspectors should observe 'how targets for individual pupils of all abilities are agreed . . .' (p. 88) ● Inspectors should take samples of students' work to see 'how assessment contributes to planning work for gifted and talented pupils . . . and how the outcomes are considered in reviews.' (p. 88)

From *Meeting the Needs of Your Most Able Pupils: Physical Education and Sport*, David Fulton Publishers 2006

Evaluation focus	Issue	Judgement/evidence
Quality of education	Teachers' command of subject	● 'Pupils should be learning from experts.' ● 'Teachers' knowledge is demonstrated in the way they . . . cater for the more able in a subject.' (p. 77)
	Appropriate challenge	● 'Effective teaching extends pupils intellectually, creatively and physically. Inspectors should judge whether teachers are determined to get the best out of the pupils and if they are being challenged enough.' (p. 78) ● Inspectors are advised to 'observe what is done to challenge the most able pupils in the class, including those who may be identified by the school as gifted and talented. Watch for those pupils who are clearly not being challenged enough. What is the effect of lack of challenge on them? Where no obvious special provision is being made, find out why.' (p. 81)
	Learning methods and resources	● Judge the approaches used for pupils of high ability.' (p. 79) ● Inspectors should assess whether 'teachers involve all pupils in lessons, giving the diffident and the slower learners a chance to contribute and time to answer questions, and yet challenging the most able.' (p. 75)
	Homework	● 'How well is homework tailored to individual needs and capabilities?' (p. 81)
	Equality of access (to the curriculum)	● 'Does it take account of their cultural background and religious beliefs, diverse ethnic backgrounds, special educational needs and particular gifts or talents?' (p. 100)
	Pupil care	● Evidence of the care of pupils will include provision for those who are gifted and talented. (p. 109)
Management	Inclusion	● Does the school provide successfully for pupils who . . . are gifted and talented?' (p. 144)
Schools causing concern	Underachieving schools	● 'Triggers that might suggest a school is underachieving include: . . . lack of challenge and slow progress for particular groups of pupils (for example the most able), in certain classes, a particular stage or in several subjects.' (p. 164)
Initiatives for raising achievement	Excellence in Cities	● 'Gifted and Talented pupils should be identified in EiC schools . . . The school should have a policy and teaching programme for these pupils. Inspectors should evaluate the effectiveness of the school's strategy in motivating gifted and talented pupils and ensuring that they achieve as well as they can both in lessons and extracurricular activities.' (p. 30)

The page numbers refer to the Ofsted *Handbook for Inspecting Secondary Schools* (2003).

From *Meeting the Needs of Your Most Able Pupils: Physical Education and Sport*, David Fulton Publishers 2006

National quality standards in gifted and talented education

A – Effective teaching and learning strategies

Generic Elements	Entry	Developing	Exemplary
1. Identification	i. The school/college has learning conditions and systems to identify gifted and talented pupils in all year groups and an agreed definition and shared understanding of the meaning of 'gifted and talented' within its own, local and national contexts	i. Individual pupils are screened annually against clear criteria at school/college and subject/topic level	i. **Multiple criteria and sources of evidence** are used to identify gifts and talents, including through the use of a broad range of quantitative and qualitative data
	ii. An **accurate record** of the identified gifted and talented population is kept and updated.	ii. The record is used to identify under-achievement and **exceptional achievement** (both within and outside the population) and to **track/review pupil progress**	ii. The record is supported by a comprehensive monitoring, progress planning and reporting system which all staff regularly share and contribute to
	iii. The identified gifted and talented population broadly reflects the school/college's **social and economic composition, gender and ethnicity**	iii. **Identification** systems address issues of **multiple exceptionality** (pupils with specific gifts/talents and special educational needs)	iii. **Identification** processes are regularly reviewed and refreshed in the light of pupil performance and value-added data. The gifted and talented population is fully representative of the school/college's population
Evidence			
Next steps			
2. Effective provision in the classroom	i. The school/college addresses the different needs of the gifted and talented population by providing a stimulating learning environment and by extending the teaching repertoire	i. Teaching and learning strategies are diverse and flexible, meeting the needs of distinct pupil groups within the gifted and talented population (e.g. able underachievers, exceptionally able)	i. The school/college has established a range of methods to find out what works best in the classroom, and shares this within the school/college and with other schools and colleges
	ii. Teaching and learning is differentiated and delivered through both individual and group activities	ii. A range of challenging learning and teaching strategies is evident in lesson planning and delivery. **Independent learning skills** are developed.	ii. Teaching and learning are suitably challenging and varied, incorporating the **breadth, depth and pace** required to progress high achievement. Pupils routinely work independently and self-reliantly

	iii. Opportunities exist to extend learning through **new technologies**	iii. The use of **new technologies** across the curriculum is focused on **personalised learning** needs	iii. The innovative use of **new technologies** raises the achievement and motivation of gifted and talented pupils
Evidence			
Next steps			
3. Standards	i. Levels of **attainment** and **achievement** for gifted and talented pupils are comparatively high in relation to the rest of the school/college population and are in line with those of similar pupils in similar schools/colleges	i. Levels of **attainment** and **achievement** for gifted and talented pupils are broadly consistent across the gifted and talented population and above those of similar pupils in similar schools/colleges	i. Levels of **attainment** and **achievement** for gifted and talented pupils indicate sustainability over time and are well above those of similar pupils in similar schools/colleges
	ii. Self-evaluation indicates that gifted and talented provision is satisfactory	ii. Self-evaluation indicates that gifted and talented provision is good	ii. Self-evaluation indicates that gifted and talented provision is very good or excellent
	iii. Schools/colleges gifted and talented education programmes are explicitly linked to the achievement of SMART outcomes and these highlight improvements in pupils' attainment and achievement		
Evidence			
Next steps			

B – Enabling curriculum entitlement and choice

4. Enabling curriculum entitlement and choice	i. Curriculum organisation is flexible, with opportunities for enrichment and increasing subject/topic choice. Pupils are provided with support and guidance in making choices	i. The curriculum offers opportunities and guidance to pupils which enable them to work beyond their age and/or phase, and across subjects or topics, according to their aptitudes and interests	i. The curriculum offers **personalised learning pathways** for pupils which maximise individual **potential**, retain flexibility of future choices, extend well beyond test/examination requirements and result in sustained impact on pupil **attainment and achievement**
Evidence			
Next steps			

Definitions for words and phrases in bold are provided in the glossary in the Quality Standards *User Guide*, available at www2.teachernet.gov.uk/gat.

© Crown copyright 2005

Generic Elements	Entry	Developing	Exemplary
C – Assessment for learning			
5. Assessment for learning	i. Processes of data analysis and pupil assessment are employed throughout the school/college to plan learning for gifted and talented pupils	i. Routine progress reviews, using both qualitative and quantitative data, make effective use of prior, predictive and value-added **attainment** data to plan for progression in pupils' learning	i. **Assessment data** are used by teachers and across the school/college to ensure challenge and sustained progression in individual pupils' learning
	ii. Dialogue with pupils provides focused feedback which is used to plan future learning	ii. Systematic oral and written feedback helps pupils to set challenging curricular targets	ii. Formative assessment and individual target-setting combine to maximise and celebrate pupils' achievements
	iii. Self and peer assessment, based on clear understanding of criteria, are used to increase pupils' responsibility for learning	iii. Pupils reflect on their own skill development and are involved in the design of their own targets and tasks	iii. Classroom practice regularly requires pupils to reflect on their own **progress** against targets, and engage in the direction of their own learning
Evidence			
Next steps			
6. Transfer and transition	i. Shared processes, using agreed criteria, are in place to ensure the productive transfer of information from one setting to another (i.e. from class to class, year to year and school/college to school/college)	i. Transfer information concerning gifted and talented pupils, including parental input, informs targets for pupils to ensure **progress** in learning. Particular attention is given to including new admissions	i. Transfer data concerning gifted and talented pupils are used to inform planning of teaching and learning at subject/aspect/topic and individual pupil level, and to ensure progression according to ability rather than age or phase
Evidence			
Next steps			
D – School/College organisation			
7. Leadership	i. A named member of the governing body, senior management team and the lead professional responsible for gifted and talented education have clearly directed responsibilities for motivating and driving gifted and talented provision. The head teacher actively champions gifted and talented provision	i. **Responsibility** for gifted and talented provision is **distributed**, and evaluation of its impact shared, at all levels in the school/college. Staff subscribe to policy at all levels. Governors play a significant supportive and evaluative role	i. Organisational structures, communication channels and the deployment of staff (e.g. workforce remodelling) are flexible and creative in supporting the delivery of **personalised learning**. Governors take a lead in celebrating achievements of gifted and talented pupils
Evidence			
Next steps			

	Entry	Developing	Exemplary
8. Policy	i. The gifted and talented policy is integral to the school/college's inclusion agenda and approach to personalised learning, feeds into and from the single school/college improvement plan and is consistent with other policies	i. The policy directs and reflects best practice in the school/college, is regularly reviewed and is clearly linked to other policy documentation	i. The policy includes input from the whole school/college community and is regularly refreshed in the light of innovative national and international practice
Evidence			
Next steps			
9. School/College ethos and pastoral care	i. The school/college sets high expectations, recognises achievement and celebrates the successes of all its pupils ii. The school/college identifies and addresses the particular social and emotional needs of gifted and talented pupils in consultation with pupils, parents and carers	i. The school/college fosters an environment which promotes positive behaviour for learning. Pupils are listened to and their views taken into account. ii. Strategies exist to counteract bullying and any adverse effects of social and curriculum pressures. Specific support for able underachievers and pupils from different cultures and social backgrounds is available and accessible	i. An ethos of ambition and achievement is agreed and shared by the whole school/college community. Success across a wide range of abilities is celebrated ii. The school/college places equal emphasis on high achievement and emotional well-being, underpinned by programmes of support personalised to the needs of gifted and talented pupils. There are opportunities for pupils to use their gifts to benefit other pupils and the wider community
Evidence			
Next steps			
10. Staff development	i. Staff have received professional development in meeting the needs of gifted and talented pupils	i. The induction programme for new staff addresses gifted and talented issues, both at whole school/college and specific subject/aspect level	i. There is **ongoing audit of staff needs** and an appropriate range of professional development in gifted and talented education. Professional development is informed by research and collaboration within and beyond the school/college

Definitions for words and phrases in bold are provided in the glossary in the Quality Standards *User Guide*, available at www2.teachernet.gov.uk/gat.
© Crown copyright 2005

121

Generic Elements	Entry	Developing	Exemplary
	ii. The lead professional responsible for gifted and talented education has received appropriate professional development	ii. Subject/aspect and phase leaders have received specific professional development in meeting the needs of gifted and talented pupils	ii. Priorities for the development of gifted and talented provision are included within a professional development entitlement for all staff and are monitored through performance management processes
Evidence			
Next steps			
11. Resources	i. Provision for gifted and talented pupils is supported by appropriate budgets and resources	i. Allocated resources include school/college based and nationally available resources, and these have a significant and measurable impact on the progress that pupils make and their attitudes to learning	i. Resources are used to stimulate innovative and experimental practice, which is shared throughout the school/college and which are regularly reviewed for impact and best value
Evidence			
Next steps			
12. Monitoring and evaluation	i. **Subject and phase audits focus on the quality** of teaching and learning for gifted and talented pupils. Whole school/college targets are set using prior **attainment data**	i. Performance against targets (including at pupil level) is regularly reviewed. Targets include qualitative pastoral and curriculum outcomes as well as numerical data	i. Performance against targets is rigorously evaluated against clear criteria. Qualitative and quantitative outcomes inform whole school/college self-evaluation processes
	ii. Elements of provision are planned against clear objectives within effective whole-school self-evaluation processes	ii. All elements, including non-academic aspects of gifted and talented provision are planned to clear objectives and are subjected to detailed evaluation	ii. The school/college examines and challenges its own provision to inform development of further experimental and innovative practice in collaboration with other schools/colleges
Evidence			
Next steps			

E – Strong partnerships beyond the school

13. Engaging with the community, families and beyond	i. Parents/carers are aware of the school's/college's policy on gifted and talented provision, contribute to its **identification** processes and are kept informed of developments in gifted and talented provision, including through the School Profile	i. Parents/carers are actively engaged in extending provision. Support for gifted and talented provision is integrated with other children's services (e.g. Sure Start, EAL, traveller, refugee, **LAC** Services)	
	ii. The school/college shares good practice and has some collaborative provision with other schools, colleges and the wider community	ii. There is strong emphasis on collaborative and innovative working with other schools/colleges which impacts on quality of provision locally, regionally and nationally	
Evidence			
Next steps			
14. Learning beyond the classroom	i. There are opportunities for pupils to learn beyond the school/college day and site (extended hours and out-of-school activities)	i. Innovative models of learning beyond the classroom are developed in collaboration with local and national schools/colleges to further enhance teaching and learning	
	ii. Pupils participate in dedicated gifted and talented activities (e.g. summer schools) and their participation is recorded	ii. Coherent strategies are used to direct and develop individual expert performance via external agencies e.g. HE/FE links, on-line support, and local/regional/national programmes	
Evidence			
Next steps			

Note (middle-progression statements as appearing in table):

i. Progression of gifted and talented pupils is enhanced by home–school/college partnerships. There are strategies to engage and support hard-to-reach parents/carers

ii. A coherent strategy for networking with other schools, colleges and local community organisations extends and enriches provision

i. A coherent programme of enrichment and extension activities (through extended hours and out-of-school activities) complements teaching and learning and helps identify pupils' latent gifts and talents

ii. Local and national provision helps meet individual pupils' learning needs e.g. NAGTY membership, accessing outreach, local enrichment programmes

Definitions for words and phrases in bold are provided in the glossary in the Quality Standards *User Guide*, available at www2.teachernet.gov.uk/gat.

Identifying talent through dynamic assessment

(from Hungerhill Comprehensive School, Doncaster)

Duration: 50 minutes
Phase in scheme: 4/8

Resources needed:

- agility ladders
- hurdles
- spots/cones
- mats
- tag belts and tags

Learning focus/outcome:

- Speed, agility, coordination and reaction times

Learning objectives: (What do you want students to know, perform, apply, etc.?)

1. All pupils should know and understand the terms speed, agility, coordination and reaction time. In relation to agility, pupils will know what directional and multi-directional pathways are and use them within the practices.
2. All pupils will perform a variety of exercises in order to improve their speed, agility, coordination and reaction times. Some pupils will have progressed further and will perform with control and consistency.
3. All pupils should be able to apply the terms speed, agility, coordination and reaction time to a practical situation and suggest how this may benefit them in terms of their performance.

Teacher objectives: (What is the focus for your development with reference to the standards and targets set?)

 From *Meeting the Needs of Your Most Able Pupils:: Physical Education and Sport*, David Fulton Publishers 2006

Indicative time	Learning objectives	Learning activity and organisation (Progressive tasks to achieve the outcome and lay-out of the activity)	Teaching points (Technical points about how to perform the skill or details about tactical aspects being taught)	Differentiation (Are all ranges of ability catered for? Have you considered, for example, groupings, task, etc.?)

10 minutes	• Set learning objectives
	• Raise heart rate
		Groups of 5, relay activities to a line and back.
		
		1. Walking on toes
		2. Ankle flicks – hop on 1 leg and turn other ankle upwards, pulling toes back towards you
		3. Skipping
		4. Jogging with right (R) knee lift – a few little steps and then lift knee
		5. Hopping and bring opposite knee inwards, across body
		6. As above but knees up and outwards
		7. Pre-turns, sideways on, 1 foot slightly in front of other, bringing knee up
		   • Dynamic stretching
		   • Stretching throughout the movement
		   • Lunges – big step forward, aim to get the back knee close to the floor
		   • still working in groups using the SAQ hurdles
			• Use arms (90 degrees) – opposite arm to leg
			• On toes, up onto balls of feet
			• Keep head up
			• Exaggerate movements
			• Fast, reactive
				• Different speed
				• Accuracy of movement
				• Vary the length and time of the exercise
				• mixed ability groups

15 minutes	• Know and understand the terms speed and coordination • Perform a variety of exercises	Lateral movement – speed and coordination – explain the terms – ask pupils questions. 1. Stepping down the side of the hurdles, sideways on; aim – to 'step over' the hurdle when you're opposite; go down 1 side, then repeat at the other 2. As above, but this time lift R leg high and over the side of the hurdle; repeat on both sides 3. Stepping over the middle of the hurdle, 1 foot then the other in between each hurdle 4. Bounding – 2-footed jumps 5. As above, add twist to the body	• Don't cross feet over • Use arms to help • On the balls of feet, and push off • Light on toes	• Speed and accuracy of movement • isolate arms for more able • go down both sides of the hurdles • Utilise demo and explanation • Reframe questions, and guide responses • Increase/decrease number of hurdles

Indicative time	Learning objectives	Learning activity and organisation	Teaching points	Differentiation
	• Know and understand the term agility • Apply the term to a practical setting – why is it useful, when would it be used?	Agility ladders. Agility – ask/ explain what agility is. When would it be used in a practical setting? 1. Running through, 1 foot in each square 2. Quick feet, 1 foot then the other in each square; practise with L and R leg lead 3. Jumping, 2 feet in square, then both out – 'in, out' 4. Jumping in the squares, 2 forward, 1 back 5. Feet in, in, out, out of ladder	• Start off slow to get the correct movement, then build the speed up gradually • Light on balls of feet • Head up	• Reframe questions • Guide responses • Utilise demo and explanation • Speed of movement • Creating new footwork patterns • Increase/ decrease length of ladder • Add a catch of a ball for the more able
5 minutes	• Know what pathways are and perform them in the practice.	Start — L leg side step — with R knee lift ____ L leg lead over each hurdle In. in. out. out 2-footed jumps ○ Agility run – zig-zag – touch each cone ○ then run back to start	• Use arms • Light on feet • Push off from outside foot	• Speed of circuit • Time the more able, and repeat to try and beat time • Add balls to catch • Use more/less equipment – ladders, hurdles, cones • Increase/decrease the length of the circuit • Use easier/harder pathways to test pupils' agility
15 minutes	• Know and understand the term reaction time • Apply the term to a practical setting – why are good reactions important? • perform a variety of reaction exercises	What is reaction time? Why is it useful? When would you need good reaction times? In groups of 5. Each group has a mat and has to react and run to the other side of the area when the teacher says 'go'. 1. Pupils lie down on their front 2. Lie down on their backs, with arms by their side, then crossed 3. Sitting cross-legged 4. Pupils in pairs, each on a mat, one in front of the other; on 'go', the back person has to try to catch the front person; both are kneeling	• Use hands to push off • Use arms • Light on feet	• Reframe questions and guide responses • Variety of different starts • Increase/decrease the length of the run • Add obstacles for pupils to go round/over • Move the mats closer/further apart • Match pupils' speed • Different speeds

Indicative time	Learning objectives	Learning activity and organisation	Teaching points	Differentiation
	• Apply all the new terms to a game situation	Two groups – competition between the groups: • Half the group has a belt and 2 tags on • Aim: group without belts have 30 seconds to try to get the tags from the other team, 1 belt at a time, and they have to be taken to the teacher • Swap the belts over so both groups experience both roles	• Use the space • Dodging – push off from outside foot • Change of pace/direction	• Increase/decrease the size of the playing area • Increase/decrease the time • mixed ability groups
5 minutes	• Cool down and plenary	Four groups (repeat warm up activities): • Little skips • Extending heel • Walk – bringing knees up high • Lunges • Static stretches Key questions	• Stretching – don't bounce, hold for 8–10 seconds • Review learning objectives: What is agility, etc.? when would it be useful in practical situations? Give specific sporting examples.	• Pick pupils to offer stretches and names of muscles • Pick pupils to answer questions • Guide responses

---

Assessment strategies: (for all abilities)

• Pre- and post-testing within the scheme
• Teacher observation
• Non-participants give feedback on performance
• Question and answer throughout the lesson
• Key plenary questions linking to learning objectives

Safety considerations:

• Check working area
• Utilise warm up
• Remove jewellery and chewing gum, etc.
• Check kit and footwear
• Check any injuries, health problems, e.g. asthma-inhalers
• Check equipment is suitable and in good condition

Cross-curricular opportunities: (e.g. National Strategies, literacy, numeracy, citizenship)

• Literacy – appropriate terminology and understanding – SAQ, speed, agility, coordination, reaction time, pathways – directional and multi-directional
• Citizenship – working with others, cooperation, teamwork
• Links to other areas of NCPE – good for athletics

ICT opportunities: (to enhance student learning, understanding and opportunities for assessment)

• In future lessons – recording of pre- and post-test results and noting the change/improvement
• Glossary of terms
• Pupils develop their own circuit

Physical assessment timetable

Physical assessment plan: Year 7 – 360 pupils

Time	Activity	Group	Location	Responsible	Safety considerations
9:00–9:15	Introduction	Group 1 boys (90) Group 1 girls (90)	Gym	All staff	• kit check • jewellery check
9:15–9:30	Warm-up: group warm-up with teacher-led movements to music	Group 1 boys (90) Group 1 girls (90)	Gym Sports hall	Head of boys' PE Head of girls' PE	• spacing • progressive intensity warm-up and static stretches
9:30–10:30	• sit and reach • standing long jump • sergeant jump • flexed arm hang • grip strength • height • weight	Group 1 boys (90)	Gym	Further education students (2 students per activity)	Follow recommended safety guidelines for each test.
9:30–10:30	Multi-stage fitness test	Group 1 girls (90)	Sports hall	Head of girls' PE	BAALPE guidelines for MSFT – Advice on safety, safe practice in PE (1999)
10:30–10:45	Break				
10:45–11:45	• sit and reach • standing long jump • sergeant jump • flexed arm hang • grip strength • height • weight	Group 1 girls (90)	Gym	Further education students (2 students per activity)	Follow recommended safety guidelines for each test.
10:45–11:45	Multi-stage fitness test	Group 1 boys (90)	Sports hall	Head of boys' PE	BAALPE guidelines for MSFT – Advice on safety, safe practice in PE (1999)

Repeat timetable for other half of Year group

 From *Meeting the Needs of Your Most Able Pupils: Physical Education and Sport*, David Fulton Publishers 2006

School honours programme example

Lymm High School: The Honours Programme 2004–2005

In order for the honours programme to be fair, the PE department have developed the criteria listed in the table below.

Award of	For	Details
School team colours	Any pupil who has represented the school on a regular basis in any year group in any school based sport.	This will be a badge that can be sewn on to the blazer below the school emblem. The colour of the badge will be blue with bronze writing i.e. football, hockey, etc. **Year 9 Hockey**
District team colours	Any pupil who has represented the district on a regular basis in any year group in any of the school based activities.	This will be a badge that can be sewn on to the blazer below the school emblem. It can be worn alongside existing badges or can replace school team colours. The colour of the badge will be blue with silver writing. **Year 9 Hockey**
County team colours	Any pupil who has represented the district (Warrington-mid Cheshire) on a regular basis in any year group in any of the school activities.	This will be a badge that can be sewn on to the blazer below the school emblem. It can be worn alongside existing badges or can replace district team colours. The colour of the badge will be blue with gold writing. **Year 9 Hockey**
Regional and national colours	Any pupil who has represented the region (north) or a country (England) in any year group in any sport.	This will be a badge that can be pinned to the blazer. It can be worn alongside existing badges or can replace county team colours if applicable. Pupils will also receive a full school sports colours tie. **Hockey**
Year 13 award	Any pupil who has represented the school in sports activities during all years of study at Lymm High School. This could also be in the form of helping staff, leading groups, volunteering at events.	Full school sports colours tie.

 From *Meeting the Needs of Your Most Able Pupils: Physical Education and Sport*, David Fulton Publishers 2006

Stages in mentoring disaffected talented pupils in PE

Flow chart representing the stages of mentoring disaffected
talented pupils in physical education

Identify pupils who demonstrate an interpersonal deficiency through:

Formative assessment
Summative assessment
Liaison with SENCO/learning mentors

Specify an initial level of responsibility with which the pupil's behaviour
matches and which area of talent is being affected

Carry out an initial observation of the pupil using the observation sheet
specifically related to the pupil's level of responsibility

Meet with the pupil to raise their awareness of the levels being used and
the stage of responsibility the pupil is at.
Identify areas for development 'working towards' and devise a self-
grading report card

Develop personal plan based on self-grading feedback

 From *Meeting the Needs of Your Most Able Pupils: Physical Education and Sport*, David Fulton Publishers 2006

Individual physical education plan

Name: **Review date:**

Class teacher: **Start date:**   **DOB:**   **Year:**

Learning mentor:

Goals to be achieved	Possible strategies	Mentor's role	Resources/techniques	Outcome

Student contribution

From *Meeting the Needs of Your Most Able Pupils: Physical Education and Sport*, David Fulton Publishers 2006

Appendix 5.2

References

Abbott, A., Collins, D., Martindale, R. and Sowerby, K. (2002) *Talent Identification and Development: An Academic Review.* Edinburgh: Sport Scotland.

Abernethy, B., Côté, J. and Baker, J. (2002) *Expert Decision-making in Team Sport.* Canberra: Australian Institute of Sport.

Assessment and Qualifications Alliance (AQA) (2006) *GCE A/AS Sport and PE* (5581, 6581). www.aqa.org.uk/qual/gceasa.html.

Bailey, R. P. (2000) 'Movement development and the primary school child', in R. P. Bailey and T. M. Macfadyen (eds), *Teaching Physical Education 5–11.* London: Continuum.

Bailey, R. P. (2001) *Teaching Physical Education.* London: Kogan Page.

Bailey, R. P. and Morley, D. (2003) 'Towards a model of talent development in physical education'. Paper presented to the British Educational Research Association Annual conference, Edinburgh.

Bailey, R. P., Tan, J. E. C. and Morley, D. (2004) 'Talented pupils in physical education: secondary teachers' experiences of the 'Excellence in Cities' scheme', *Physical Education and Sport Pedagogy,* **9** (2), 133–48.

Bailey, R. P., Morley, D. and Dismore, H. (2005) 'A national audit of talent development policies and practice in England'. Paper presented to the British Educational Research Association annual conference, University of Glamorgan, Cardiff.

Bailey, R. P. and Morley, D. (forthcoming) 'Towards a model of talent development in physical education'. *Sport, Education and Society.*

Baker, J. and Horton, S. (2004) 'A review of primary and secondary influences on sport expertise', *High Ability Studies,* **15**, 211–28.

Baker, J., Côté, J. and Abernathy, B. (2003) 'Sport specific training, deliberate practice and the development of expertise in team ball sports', *Journal of Applied Sport Psychology,* **15**, 12–25.

Balyi, I. (2001) *Sport System Building and Long-Term Athlete Development in British Columbia.* Vancouver: SportsMed BC.

Balyi, I. and Hamilton, A. (2000) 'Key to success: long-term athlete development', *Sport Coach,* **23** (1), 10–32.

Beashel, P. (2002) 'Physical education', in D. Eyre and H. Lowe (2002) *Curriculum Provision for the Gifted and Talented in Secondary School.* London: David Fulton.

Benn, C. and Chitty, C. (1996) *Thirty Years On: Is Comprehensive Education Alive and Well or Struggling to Survive?* London: David Fulton.

Bloom, B.S. (ed.) (1985) *Developing Talent in Young People.* New York: Ballantine Books.

Burton, A. and Miller, D. (1998) *Movement Skill Assessment.* Leeds: Human Kinetics.

Cale, L. and Harris, J. (2002) 'National fitness testing for children: issues, concerns and alternatives', *British Journal of Teaching Physical Education,* **33** (1), 32.

Cale, L. and Harris, J. (eds) (2005) *Exercise and Young People: Issues, Implications and Initiatives.* Palgrave Macmillan: Basingstoke.

Campbell, R. J., Eyre, D., Muijs, R. D., Neelands, J. G. A. and Robinson, W. (2004) *The English Model: Context, Policy and Challenge.* www.nagty.ac.uk/expertise_centre/downloadable_materials/index.aspx.

Ceci, S. (1991). 'How much does schooling influence general intelligence and its cognitive components? A reassessment of the evidence', *Developmental Psychology,* **27**, 703–22.

Côté, J. (1999) 'The influence of the family in the development of talent in sports', *The Sports Psychologist,* **13**, 395–417.

Côté, J. and Hay, J. (2002). 'Children's involvement in sport: a developmental analysis', in J. M. Silva and D. Stevens (eds) *Psychological Foundations of Sport.* Boston, MA: Allyn and Bacon.

Côté, J., Baker, J. and Abernethy, B. (2003) 'From play to practice: a developmental framework for the acquisition of expertise in team sports', in: J. L. Starkes and K.A. Ericsson (eds) *Expert Performance in Sport: Advances in Research on Sport Expertise.* Champaign, IL: Human Kinetics.

Cropley, A. J. (1995) 'Actualizing creative intelligence', in J. Freeman, P. Span and H. Wagner (eds) *Actualizing Talent: A Lifelong Challenge.* London: Cassell.

Csikszentmihalyi, M. (1975) *Beyond Boredom and Anxiety.* San Francisco: Jossey-Bass.

Department for Culture, Media and Sport (2005a) *Living Life to the Full.* London: DCMS.

DCMS (2005b) *Business Plan 2005.* London: DCMS.

Department for Education and Employment (1997) *Excellence in Schools.* London: TSO.

DfEE (1999a) *Excellence in Cities.* London: DfEE.

DfEE (1999b) *National Curriculum for Physical Education.* London: DfEE.

DfEE (2000) *Excellence in Cities: Report March 1999–September 2000.* London: DFEE.

Department for Education and Skills (2001) *Schools Achieving Success.* London: DfES.

DfES (2002) *Excellence in Cities Homepage.* www.standards.dfes.gov.uk/excellence (accessed 10/05/02).

DfES/DCMS (2003) *Learning Through PE and Sport.* London: DfES/DCMS.

DfES/DCMS (2004) *The Impact of School Sport Partnerships: The Results of the 2003/04 PE, School Sport and Club Links Survey.* London: DfES.

Ennis, C. D. (1999) 'Creating a culturally relevant curriculum for disengaged girls', *Sport, Education and Society,* **4** (1), 31–49.

Eyre, D. (2001) *Able Children in Ordinary Schools.* London: David Fulton.

Eyre, D. and Lowe, H. (2002) *Curriculum Provision for the Gifted and Talented in Secondary School.* London: David Fulton.

Fisher, R. (1996) 'Gifted children and young people in physical education and sport', in N. Armstrong (ed.) *New Directions in Physical Education – Change and Innovation.* London: Cassell.

Freeman, J. (1991) *Gifted Children Growing Up.* London: Cassell.

Freeman, J. (1998) *Educating the Very Able: Current International Research.* London: Ofsted.

Freeman, J. (2001) *Gifted Children Grown Up.* London: David Fulton.

Gagné, F. (2000) 'Understanding the complex choreography of talent development through DMGT-based analysis', in K. A. Heller, F. J. Mönks, R. J. Sternberg and R. F. Subotnik (eds) *International Handbook of Giftedness and Talent* (second edition). Oxford: Elsevier.

Gallahue, D. L. (1982) *Fundamental Movement Experiences for Children.* New York: Wiley.

Gallahue, D. L. and Ozmun, J. C. (1998) *Understanding Motor Development: Infants, Children, Adolescents, Adult* (fifth edition). Boston, MA: McGraw-Hill.

Gardner, H. (1980) *Artful Scribbles.* New York: Basic Books.

Gardner, H. (1983) *Frames of Mind.* New York: Basic Books.

Gay, B. and Richardson, J. (1998) 'The mentoring dilemma: guidance and/or direction?' *Mentoring and Tutoring,* **6** (1/2), 43–53.

George, D. (2003) *Gifted Education: Identification and Provision* (second edition). London: David Fulton.

Grabiner, M. and McKelvain, R. (1985) 'Implementation of a profiling/prediction test battery in the screening of elite men gymnasts', in B. Petiot, J. H. Salmela and T. B. Hoshizaki (eds) *World Identification Systems for Gymnastic Talent.* Montreal: Sport Psyche Editions.

Greenberg, M. T., Kusche, C. A., Cook, E. T. and Quamma, J. P. (1995). 'Promoting emotional competence in school-aged children: the effects of the PATHS curriculum', *Development and Psychopathology,* **7**, 117–36.

Gunnell, S. (1995) *Running Tall.* London: Bloomsbury.

Hands, B. (2002) 'How can we best measure fundamental movement skills?' ACHPER Interactive Health and Physical Education Conference. University of Tasmania, Launceston Campus, 3–6 July 2002.

Heller, F. K. A., Mönks, J., Sternberg, R. J. and Subotnik, R. F. (eds) (2000) *International Handbook of Giftedness and Talent* (second edition). Oxford: Elsevier.

Hellison, D. (2003) *Teaching responsibility through physical activity* (second edition). Champaign, IL: Human Kinetics.

Holt, N. L. and Morley, D. (2004) 'Gender differences in Psychosocial factors associated with athletic success during childhood', *The Sport Psychologist,* **18**, 138–53.

Hymer, B. and Michel, D. (2002) *Gifted and Talented Learners: Creating a policy for inclusion.* London: NACE/Fulton.

Jess, M. and Collins, D. (2003) 'Primary physical education in Scotland: the future in the making', *European Journal of Physical Education,* **8** (2) 103–18.

Johnson, M. (2003) *Martin Johnson: The Autobiography.* London: Headline.

Kane, J. E. (1986) 'Giftedness in sport', in G. Gleeson (ed) *The Growing Child in Competitive Sport.* London: Hodder and Stoughton.

Kay, T. (1995) *Women and Sport: A Review of Research.* London: The Sports Council.

Keeves, J. P. (1988) 'Models and model building', in J. P. Keeves (ed) *Educational Research, Methodology and Measurement: An International Handbook*. Oxford: Pergamon.

Kimble, G. A. (1993) 'Evolution of the nature–nurture issue in the history of psychology', in R. Plomin and G. E. McClearn (eds), *Nature, Nurture, and Psychology*. Washington DC: American Psychological Association.

Kirk, D. and Gorely, T. (2000) 'Challenging thinking about the relationship between physical education and sporting performance', *European Physical Education Review*, 6, 119–34.

Kirk, D., Brettschnieder, W. and Auld, C. (2003) 'Junior sports models representing best practice nationally and internationally'. Paper prepared for the Australian Sport Commission, March, 2003.

Kirschenbaum, R. J. (1998) 'Dynamic assessment and its use with underserved gifted and talented populations', *Gifted Child Quarterly*, 42, 140–7.

Kohn, M. (1995) *The Race Gallery: The Return of Racial science*. London: Jonathan Cape.

Macfadyen, T. and Bailey, R. P. (2002) *Teaching Physical Education 11–18*. London: Continuum.

Montgomery, D. (2000) *Able Underachievers*. London: Whurr.

Moore, P., Collins, D., Burwitz, L. and Jess, M. (1998) *The Development of Talent Study (DOTS)*. London: English Sports Council.

Morley, D. and Bailey, R. P. (2004) 'Talent identification and provision in physical education: a strategic approach', *British Journal of Teaching Physical Education*, 35, 41–4.

Morley, D., Bailey, R. P. and Holt, N. L. (2003) 'Teachers' perceptions of talent in physical education'. Paper presented at the British Educational Research Association conference, Edinburgh.

Mosston, M. and Ashworth, S. (1986) *Teaching Physical Education*. Toronto: Merrill.

Murdoch, E. B. (1990) 'Physical education and sport: the interface', in N. Armstrong (ed) *New Directions in Physical Education*. London: Cassell.

O'Connor, J. and Seymour, J. (2003) *Introducing NLP Neuro-Linguistic Programming*. London: HarperCollins.

Ofsted (2001) *Guidance to Inspectors – The Identification and Provision for Gifted and Talented Pupils*. London: Office for Standards in Education.

Ofsted (2003) *Expecting the Unexpected: Developing Creativity In Primary And Secondary Schools. A Summary of Ofsted Report*. HMI 1612, August 2003.

Ofsted (2004) *Provision for Gifted and Talented Pupils in Physical Education: 2003–2004*. London: TSO.

Okely, A, D., Booth, M. L. and Patterson, J, W. (2001) 'Relationship of physical activity to fundamental movement skills among adolescents', *Medicine in science and Sport Exercise*, 33 (11), 1899–904.

Penney, D. (2000) 'Physical education, sporting excellence and educational excellence', *European Physical Educational Review*, 6, 135–50.

Perleth, C. and Heller, K. A. (1994) 'The Munich longitudinal study of giftedness', in R. F. Subotnik and K. D. Arnold (eds) *Beyond Terman*. Norwood, NJ: Ablex.

Perleth, C., Schatz, T. and Mönks, F. J. (2000) 'Early identification of high ability', in K. A. Heller, F. J. Mönks, R. J. Sternberg and R. F. Subotnik (eds) *International Handbook of Giftedness and Talent* (second edition). Oxford: Elsevier.

QCA/DFEE (2000) *Physical Education: A Scheme of Work for Key Stages 3 and 4*. London: QCA.

QCA (2005) *Physical Education and School Sport Case Studies*. www.qca.org.uk.

Pinker, S. (2002) *The Blank Slate: The Modern Denial of Human Nature*. New York: Viking Penguin.

Rankinen, T., Pérusse, L., Rauramaa, R., Rivera, M. A., Wolfarth, B. and Bouchard, C. (2002) 'The human gene map for performance and health-related fitness phenotypes: the 2001 update', *Medicine and science in Sports and Exercise*, 34, 1219–33.

Raudsepp, L. and Paasuke, M. (1995) 'Gender differences in fundamental movement patterns, movement performances, and strength measurements in prepubertal children', *Pediatric Exercise Science*, 7, 294–304.

Redgrave, S. (2000) *Steve Redgrave: A Golden Age*. London: BBC Books.

Regnier, G., Salmela, J. H. and Russell, S. J. (1993) 'Talent detection and development in sport', in R. N. Singer, M. Murphy and L. K. Tennant (eds) *Handbook on Research on Sport Psychology*. New York: Macmillan.

Renzulli, J. S. (1977) 'Enrichment triad model: a guide for developing defensible programs for the gifted and talented', in C. Clark and R. Callow (2002) *Educating the Gifted and Talented: Resource Issues and Processes for Teachers*. London: NACE/Fulton.

Renzulli, J. S. (1986) 'The three-ring conception of giftedness: a developmental model for creative productivity', in R. Sternberg and J. Davidson (eds) *Conceptions of giftedness*. New York: Cambridge University Press.

Rowlands, P. (1974) *Gifted Children and their Problems*. London: Dent and Sons.

Rowley, S. R. W. (1992) *Training of Young Athletes (TOYA) and the Identification of talent*. London: Sports Council.

Schoon, I. (2000) 'A life span approach to talent development', in K. A. Heller, F. J. Mönks, R. J. Sternberg and R. F. Subotnik (eds) *International Handbook of Giftedness and Talent* (second edition). Oxford: Elsevier.

Seefeldt, V., Haubenstricker, J. and Reuschlein, S. (1979) 'Why Physical Education in elementary school curriculum?', in Abbott, A., Collins, D., Martindale, R. and Sowerby, K. (2002) *Talent Identification and Development: An Academic Review*. Edinburgh: Sport Scotland.

Select Committee on Education and Employment (1998) *Highly Able Children*. London: United Kingdom Parliament.

Sherwood, K. (2005) 3 September, 2005. *Re: multi-skill club information*. E-mail to D. Morley.

Siedentop, D., Hastie, P. A. and Van Der Mars, H. (2004) *The Complete Guide to Sport Education*. Champaign, IL: Human Kinetics.

Simonton, D. (1998) *Origins Of Genius*. Oxford: Oxford University Press.

Singer, R. N. (1982) *The Learning of Motor Skills*. New York: Macmillan.

Sloane, K. and Sosniak, L. (1985) 'The development of accomplished sculptors', in B. S. Bloom (ed.) *Developing Talent in Young People*. New York: Ballantine Books, pp. 90–138.

Smith, M. (2005) (mattsmith@youthsporttrust.co.uk) 5 September 2005. Re: multi-skill academy information. E-mail to D. Morley (d.morley@leesmet.ac.uk).

Sport England (2005) Active Schools website. www.sportengland.org.

Sportscoach UK (2005) *Newsletter 15*. www.sportscoachuk.org.

Starkes, J. L. and Ericsson, K. A. (2003) *Expert Performance in Sport: Advances in Research on Sport Expertise*. Champaign, IL: Human Kinetics.

Steiner, I. D. (1972) *Group Processes and Productivity*. New York: Academic Press.

Stephenson, J. and Taylor, M. A. (1995) *Diverse Views of the Mentoring Process in Initial Teacher Training. Diversity in Mentoring*. Michigan: IMA.

Sternberg, R. J. (2000) 'Giftedness as developing expertise', in K. A. Heller, F. J. Mönks, R. J. Sternberg and R. F. Subotnik (eds) *International Handbook of Giftedness and Talent*, second edition. Oxford: Elsevier. pp. 55–66.

Stiehl, J. (1993) 'Becoming responsible: theoretical and practical considerations', *Journal of Physical Education, Recreation, and Dance*, 64 (5), 38–40, 57–59, 70–71.

Tannenbaum, A. J. (1983) *Gifted Children*. New York: Macmillan.

Teachernet (2005) *National Competition Manager's Framework*. www.teachernet.co.uk.

Tilsley, P. (1995) 'The use of tests and test data in identification or recognition of high ability', *Flying High*, 2, 43–50.

Tinning, R., Kirk, D. and Evans, J. (1993) *Learning to Teach Physical Education*. Sydney: Prentice Hall.

Tremere, R., Morley, D. and Bailey, R. P. *Utilising a Case Study Methodology to Describe and Evaluate Talent Development Strategies in Physical Education*. Paper presented to the British Educational Research Association annual conference, University of Glamorgan, Cardiff.

Van Buerden, E., Zask, A., Barnett, L, M. and Dietrich, U. C. (2002) 'Fundamental movement skills – how do primary school children perform? The "Move it Groove it" program in rural Australia', *Journal of Science and Medicine in Sport*, 5 (3), 244–252.

Vereijken, B. and Bongaardt, R. (1999) 'Complex motor skill acquisition', in Y. Vanden Auweele, F. Bakker, S. Biddle, M. Durand and R. Seiler (eds) *Psychology for Physical Educators*. Champaign, Ill: Human Kinetics. pp. 233–256.

Walkley, J., Holland, B., Treloar, R. and Probyn-Smith, H. (1993) 'Fundamental motor skill proficiency of children', *ACPHER National Journal*, 40 (3) 11–14.

West Yorkshire Sport (2005) *Multi-skills Club Guidance*. www.westyorkshiresport.co.uk.

Whitehead, M. and Maude, P. (2003) *Observing Children Moving CD ROM*. Tacklesport Consultancy.

Winner, E. (1996) *Gifted Children*. New York: Basic Books.

Wright, S. C. and Smith, D. E. (2000) 'A case for formalised mentoring', *Quest*, 52, 200–213.

Youth Sport Trust (2004) *Multi-skill Academies for Gifted and Talented pupils – Information and Guidance.* Loughborough: Youth Sport Trust.

Youth Sport Trust (2005) Junior Athlete Education Programme. www. talentladder.org.uk.